Songs of the Vineyard

Sixty-six Meditations on Isaiah

Songs of the Vineyard

Sixty-six Meditations on Isaiah

Russell C. Lambert

www.emeraldhouse.com

Songs of the Vineyard

66 Meditations on Isaiah

Printed in the United States of America

ISBN 978-1-932307-73-3

Cover design & Page Layout by David Siglin of A&E Media
Author photograph by Clark J. Lambert

AMBASSADOR INTERNATIONAL
427 Wade Hampton Blvd.
Greenville, SC 29609, USA
www.emeraldhouse.com

AMBASSADOR PUBLICATIONS
A division of
Ambassador Productions Ltd.
Providence House
Ardenlee Street
Belfast
BT6 8QJ
Northern Ireland
www.ambassador-productions.com

The colophon is a trademark of Ambassador

This book is published in association with
Patti M. Hummel, President & Agent
The Benchmark Group LLC, Nashville, TN
benchmarkgroup1@aol.com

Dedication

This is dedicated to everyone who has a heart like David's in Psalm 143: 5 & 6 *"I remember the days of old; I meditate on all thy works; I muse on the work of thy hands. I stretch forth my hands unto thee: my soul thirsteth after thee, as a thirsty land."* May the blessings of the Lord be upon you. And dedicated to my loving wife. With her skills as a proofreader, she has spent countless hours correcting my grammar, punctuation, and spelling, even when I knew I was right. Her patience and love toward me over these decades is more than I could have ever hoped for.

Table of Contents

Meditation One

Rebellion Against God

Hear, O heavens, and give ear, O earth: for the LORD hath spoken, I have nourished and brought up children, and they have rebelled against me. The ox knoweth his owner, and the ass his master's crib: but Israel doth not know, my people doth not consider. Ah sinful nation, a people laden with iniquity, a seed of evildoers, children that are corrupters: they have forsaken the LORD, they have provoked the Holy One of Israel unto anger… Isaiah 1:2-4e

Everything in nature speaks of a creator. As Christians we recognize the creator as God the Father, the first person of the Trinity. In that recognition we embrace the fact that God created mankind, humanity in His image. We have, as a race, been looked after, nourished, taken care of and brought up as His children. Even if our Bible did not tell us specifically, it would be self evident that the entire human race has rebelled against God. We have rebelled against His laws, against His authority, even denying Him as creator. How is it that we can be so irrational as to not recognize God for who He is. We are given examples of the ox and the ass, which are certainly not the smartest animals in the world. We use the phrases *dumb as an ox* or *stubborn as a jackass* and yet even they recognize their owners, unlike the nations and races of men, who do not take the time to know or consider their position to, or relationship with, God. Even those of us who call Him Father often times lack a contemplative attitude towards Him. Israel is told to consider itself as a whole. Can we do any less than realize that we too are a nation, a people, which are weighted down with a multitude of sins? A country of wicked evildoers, children who have both despised and corrupted the truth, if we are to change, to grow, we must first recognize and admit to the problem. The problem is that we have left God and we will never look for the way back until we admit we are lost.

Meditation Two

The Way of Law

And it shall come to pass in the last days, that the mountain of the LORD'S house shall be established in the top of the mountains, and shall be exalted above the hills; and all nations shall flow unto it. And many people shall go and say, Come ye, and let us go up to the mountain of the LORD, to the house of the God of Jacob; and he will teach us of his ways, and we will walk in his paths: for out of Zion shall go forth the law, and the word of the LORD from Jerusalem. And he shall judge among the nations, and shall rebuke many people: and they shall beat their swords into plowshares, and their spears into pruninghooks: nation shall not lift up sword against nation, neither shall they learn war any more. Isaiah 2:2-4

In times of war we look for peace. In times of injustice we long for righteousness. In times of anarchy we seek order. You, like myself, probably grieve over the poverty, destruction, political corruption, disease and genocide all over the world. It touches each of our lives in one way or another. And even though we may have different ideas of how we believe it should come about, most of us have a desire for a utopian society. Since I was a child I have thought of the irony of the last part of verse 4, "*and they shall beat their swords into plowshares, and their spears into pruninghooks: nation shall not lift up sword against nation, neither shall they learn war any more.*" The irony, of course, is that these words are engraved in front of the United Nations. Do we, as a people, really believe in our arrogance and pride that a society like this one can be brought about by our own efforts? Especially when we consider our history on this planet. Yet, we are given the assurance that some day it shall come to pass. It shall be brought about and established when the Lord returns as promised, to set up His earthly Kingdom. It will be a time when instead of all roads leading to Rome, all roads will lead to Jesus, a time when all peoples of the world will travel the road of pilgrimage seeking to learn the ways and teachings of Christ. But, oh so much more, for not only will His ways be sought out, but finally people will actually want to follow them. At long last peace and justice shall rule over the world and the only law shall be the law of God.

Meditation Three

The Righteous and the Wicked

Say ye to the righteous, that it shall be well with him: for they shall eat the fruit of their doings. Woe unto the wicked! it shall be ill with him: for the reward of his hands shall be given him. Isaiah 3:10-11

All of the sins of the nation and its people have been laid out before them, along with some of the consequences of those sins. As a history buff, I recognize that these are the same sins and consequences that have faced every nation just before its fall. If you take the time to read the entire chapter you will find the parallels between the United States and Judah to be so uncanny that they are eerie. The state of the government, youth and women in society, the moral depravity, disease and sickness, even attitudes and styles of apparel are represented. But right in the middle of all this is hope. The hope, of course, is for those who are holding on to God and His ways. Often times, we become discouraged by the things that go on around us. Of course, we know in our hearts that God is in control, and that He cares for all who call Him Lord. Yet, our eyes and ears see and hear something all together different. In the midst of all the turmoil, strife, and chaos, when everything seems to be on a roller coaster ride to hell, we are reminded everything will be all right for those who love the Lord and are found in Him. We find encouragement to "keep on keeping on" to do the right thing, to do the righteous thing and if we will do this we will reap the fruit of our labors, the rewards of our work. Right now that may be running counter to your senses. It almost seems that "no good deed goes unpunished" and that evil is rewarded. Yet, God is true, holy and righteous and you have not been forgotten. God sees all, hears all and knows all and in so seeing, hearing, and knowing, He assures us that "what goes around comes around."

Meditation Four

Washed Away

When the Lord shall have washed away the filth of the daughters of Zion, and shall have purged the blood of Jerusalem from the midst thereof by the spirit of judgment, and by the spirit of burning. And the LORD will create upon every dwelling place of mount Zion, and upon her assemblies, a cloud and smoke by day, and the shining of a flaming fire by night: for upon all the glory shall be a defence. Isaiah 4: 4 & 5

What strong verses these appear to be, yet, they are things that poets write about and odes are sung to. Perhaps you can recall a line from an old hymn that will give us some context, "*What can wash away my sin? Nothing but the blood of Jesus.*" Sometimes we forget that Jesus died for all the sins of all the sinners of the world, including the Jews. Keep in mind, too, that this is still in a future that you and I have not seen, a future filled with unspeakable horrors and yet a glorious promise of hope. Hope for the nation of Israel and hope for the world, a time of redemption and renewal. Another verse from the New Testament also adds to our understanding, *Matthew 3:11 "I indeed baptize you with water unto repentance: but he that cometh after me is mightier than I, whose shoes I am not worthy to bear: he shall baptize you with the Holy Ghost, and with fire:"* And so both the washing and the burning come from Jesus. Perhaps you will remember from the Exodus that God led the children of Israel through the wilderness with a cloud by day and a pillar of fire by night. Not only did the glory of God give them direction but it also gave them security, knowing that God was with them. Finally, it would serve as a warning to potential enemies to stay away from the chosen people. We have nothing to be jealous about concerning Israel's past or their future. You see, that same guidance, security and protection are offered to each and everyone who will believe in Jesus Christ as Lord and Savior today. Except that instead of being an outward manifestation it is an inward transformation brought about by the Holy Spirit of God.

Meditation Five

Song of the Vineyard

Now will I sing to my wellbeloved a song of my beloved touching his vineyard. My wellbeloved hath a vineyard in a very fruitful hill: And he fenced it, and gathered out the stones thereof, and planted it with the choicest vine, and built a tower in the midst of it, and also made a winepress therein: and he looked that it should bring forth grapes, and it brought forth wild grapes. What could have been done more to my vineyard, that I have not done in it? wherefore, when I looked that it should bring forth grapes, brought it forth wild grapes? Isaiah 5:1, 2 & 4

This is the song of the vineyard. It is said that in Hebrew this in one of the most beautiful forlorn songs in the Bible. In this melody, Israel is referred to as a vineyard planted by God. Planted in rich fertile soil, everything that could be considered a hindrance was removed. The vineyard was sheltered. There was even a winepress built on site so once the fruit had ripened into succulent grapes the juice could be extracted and shared with others bringing mirth and joy into their lives. But instead of getting big, ripe, plump, sweet, juicy grapes, what the Lord got was wild grapes, small, hard, tart and dry. And so the rhetorical question is asked, "Was there anything else I could have done that I did not do?" So what does this have to do with you and I today as Christians? Much indeed, for as Gentiles have we not been grafted in by grace through faith in Jesus Christ? Have we not been planted in fertile soil, we certainly have had all the rocks of sin removed from our lives, "the hour we first believed." We have been watered by the Holy Spirit through the fountain springing up within us. We, too, have been protected and watched over by the mighty hand of God. I pray that we have ripened into plump, sweet, juicy grapes so that when we are squeezed the nectar flows out and brings joy to those around us. And yet it is sad to say that all too often we, too, produce grapes that are small, hard, tart, and dry. And the rhetorical question for us is what more could Jesus have done than sacrifice Himself on the cross of Calvary?

Meditation Six

Undone

Then said I, Woe is me! for I am undone; because I am a man of unclean lips, and I dwell in the midst of a people of unclean lips: for mine eyes have seen the King, the LORD of hosts. Also I heard the voice of the Lord, saying, Whom shall I send, and who will go for us? Then said I, Here am I; send me. Isaiah 6:5 & 8

Imagine for a moment what it would be like to stand before Jesus in all His heavenly glory, in your current natural state. One day, of course, we will, but it will be in our glorified bodies. We don't seem to understand, even as Christians, that the closer we get to God the more we realize how bad off we are. It took the Apostle Paul his entire Christian life to learn this. At the start of his ministry he proclaimed himself to be the "least among the saints" very humble in deed for a former member of the Jewish ruling body. And yet, as he grew in his relationship with Christ and came to the end of his ministry he purports to be the "chiefest among sinners." When we get close to God we cannot stand on any kind of pretence. And so it was with Isaiah. Have you come to the realization that you are a person of unclean lips? Perhaps you don't use profanity. I hope that you don't but have you ever gossiped, said hurtful things to someone, hollered at your spouse, your children, your parents etc? Do you understand that you go to church with a bunch of people who have unclean lips? I bet you do. When you fully understand that to stand before Christ is to be undone then you can allow Him to cleanse you as by fire. Undone? What are some other ways to express I am undone? I have sinned, I am miserable, I am pierced through, I am struck dumb, I am destroyed, I am ruined and I perish. Having been cleansed you can hear Jesus say, "Whom shall I send and who will go for us?" Being cleansed and hearing the question only then can you provide the correct response, "Here am I; send me."

Meditation Seven

The Sign

Ask thee a sign of the LORD thy God; ask it either in the depth, or in the height above. But Ahaz said, I will not ask, neither will I tempt the LORD. And he said, Hear ye now, O house of David; Is it a small thing for you to weary men, but will ye weary my God also? Therefore the Lord himself shall give you a sign; Behold, a virgin shall conceive, and bear a son, and shall call his name Immanuel. Butter and honey shall he eat, that he may know to refuse the evil, and choose the good. Isaiah 7:11-15

The whole Bible is filled with signs and wonders, and promises for those who would believe the Lord. We should remember that it is not disrespectful or tempting to believe in something God has promised to us. Often times, as frail humans, we must come to the Lord and be reminded that He will not put more on us than we can bear, or that He will be with us even until the end of the world, or even that He will pour out a blessing on us if we give and tithe with an open heart. Is it not hypocritical then to trust in the Lord for our salvation but not for our physical needs? King Ahaz must have thought he sounded so pious when he remembered a verse from Sabbath School, "Ye shall not tempt the Lord your God." I guess he forgot the one about not sacrificing your children to false gods and not serving idols. God gave Ahaz a sign anyway, but not just for Ahaz alone but a sign for the nation, and for the world for all time. Would not Ahaz need a sign he could relate to? Perhaps Isaiah did marry a virgin and have a child. Often times, the Bible gives us a near, partial, fulfillment of prophesies along with a far, complete, fulfillment. Personally I trust Saint Matthew, when he wrote in *Matthew 1:22 & 23 "Now all this was done, that it might be fulfilled which was spoken of the Lord by the prophet, saying, Behold, a virgin shall be with child, and shall bring forth a son, and they shall call his name Emmanuel, which being interpreted is, God with us."*

Meditation Eight

Sanctify the Lord

Sanctify the LORD of hosts himself; and let him be your fear, and let him be your dread. And he shall be for a sanctuary; but for a stone of stumbling and for a rock of offence to both the houses of Israel, for a gin and for a snare to the inhabitants of Jerusalem. And when they shall say unto you, Seek unto them that have familiar spirits, and unto wizards that peep, and that mutter: should not a people seek unto their God? for the living to the dead? To the law and to the testimony: if they speak not according to this word, it is because there is no light in them. Isaiah 8:13, 14, 19 & 20

Today just as then, there is a lot of fear and dread in our lives, wars, evil people, the rising cost of living, losing our jobs, our health, and our homes. Still with all the fear that surrounds us and permeates our very being we are told to sanctify the Lord of Hosts in our hearts. Our only concern should be humility, reverence and service to God. If we will do that, the Lord will be our sanctuary, a place of protection and safety, of calm assurance from the storms of life around us. But for those who refuse, the Lord becomes a stumbling stone. Stumbling stone sounds familiar doesn't it? That's because Peter used this terminology in *I Peter 2:8* and Paul in *Romans 9:32 & 33.* This same principle applies today. If we put Jesus first in our lives, whom then should we be afraid of? It is ironic that even with a prohibition against it, even Christians, whether in ignorance, or willful rebellion, will seek out chandlers, wizards, and fortunetellers, trying to learn about the future by consulting with the dead. In times of distress, should we not seek the Lord our God, our Savior, the lover of our souls for solace and for guidance? Should we not go to the precious Word of God for our answers to the problems of life? Christian, beware of wolves in sheep's clothing, if anyone directs you to do these things that are contrary to the Word of God it is because the light of God is not in them.

Meditation Nine

The Deity of Christ

For unto us a child is born, unto us a son is given: and the government shall be upon his shoulder: and his name shall be called Wonderful, Counsellor, The mighty God, The everlasting Father, The Prince of Peace. Of the increase of his government and peace there shall be no end, upon the throne of David, and upon his kingdom, to order it, and to establish it with judgment and with justice from henceforth even for ever. The zeal of the LORD of hosts will perform this. Isaiah 9:6 & 7

Since the mid 1970's there has been a new fervor to strip Jesus of His deity leaving Him only a perfect Son of God but not truly God Himself come in the flesh. Yet, in this verse we clearly recognize that God is to be born as a child and be the Christ. Isaiah attributes five names to this child, Jesus; two expressing attributes Wonderful and Counselor, and three expressing deity, the Mighty God, the Everlasting Father, and the Prince of Peace. So it's true then, God did become man and dwelt among us. The teaching of the Trinity is such a precious doctrine. Just because we have difficulty understanding all of its ramifications and nuances doesn't mean that we should deny its truth. That's why when we pray, we pray to the Father, through the Son, in the Spirit. It also doesn't take any stretch of the imagination to see that there will be an eternal spiritual country that our Lord and Savior will govern over. Along with the physical Kingdom He will govern over while being seated on the throne of David in Israel, in Jerusalem. The government Jesus is seated on shall have no boundaries and the peace of His government shall be eternal. It is a Kingdom in which order prevails and righteous, holy justice is the order of the day. And it is a day without end. The earthly government shall be accomplished with the same passion, the same zeal, which caused Jesus to drive the moneychangers from the Temple on both occasions, the zeal of the Holy Spirit.

Meditation Ten

Bad Boys

Woe unto them that decree unrighteous decrees, and that write grievousness which they have prescribed; To turn aside the needy from judgment, and to take away the right from the poor of my people, that widows may be their prey, and that they may rob the fatherless! And what will ye do in the day of visitation, and in the desolation which shall come from far? to whom will ye flee for help? and where will ye leave your glory? Isaiah 10:1-3

What a stern warning this is to the judiciary, legislative and executive branches of government, to all those in authority who issue any type of decision, decree, or legislation, no person or party is excluded. In a nation founded on Judeo-Christian principals, seeking the freedom to worship Jesus in their own way, a country the United States Supreme Court declared Christian, is it not the responsibility of every judge, and politician to reflect the justice of God in society, not its depraved cultural mores? Greed and injustice permeate our society. People who need our care and consideration the most, widows and orphans, seem to receive the least. Is wealth built on the backs of the rich or on the backs of the working poor? Do the poor or the working-class really receive the same due process as the rich or famous? This foreboding warning is directed squarely at those in power. Where are you going to run when a righteous Holy God visits His judgment, His final decree, and His prescription on you? All the power and all the glory you have now, what will happen to it then? Least we forget, this is not a woe directed at those seeking the face of God who are diligently trying to do the right thing, walking and living in God's Word. Remember, too, that we are all under the watchful eye and the strong arm of God.

Meditation Eleven

The Zoo

The wolf also shall dwell with the lamb, and the leopard shall lie down with the kid; and the calf and the young lion and the fatling together; and a little child shall lead them. And the cow and the bear shall feed; their young ones shall lie down together: and the lion shall eat straw like the ox. And the sucking child shall play on the hole of the asp, and the weaned child shall put his hand on the cockatrice' den. They shall not hurt nor destroy in all my holy mountain: for the earth shall be full of the knowledge of the LORD, as the waters cover the sea. Isaiah 11:6-9

Have you ever wondered what the world was like before man surrendered to sin by wanting to become God? Have you ever thought about what the conditions must have been like before God cursed all of creation on account of mankind's sin? Here we see a small snapshot, a tiny glimpse of the world restored from the curse of the fall. Once again, harmony will reign supreme among the animal kingdom. The carnivores will be given a new set of teeth; they will eat the grass of the field just as they did in the Garden of Eden. And these wild beasts shall be as domesticated as the family lap dog, for a small child shall lead them around. Can you imagine letting your child play on the den of a cobra? It seems though; serpents will not get their legs back. Perhaps in part to remind them and us of the role they once played in the fall of man, and as a consequence of sin for allowing themselves to be possessed by the devil. Nowhere in the Lord's Millennial Kingdom will anything hurt another, for His peace and knowledge shall cover the earth like a sea.

Meditation Twelve

Wells of Salvation

And in that day thou shalt say, O LORD, I will praise thee: though thou wast angry with me, thine anger is turned away, and thou comfortedst me. Behold, God is my salvation; I will trust, and not be afraid: for the LORD JEHOVAH is my strength and my song; he also is become my salvation. Therefore with joy shall ye draw water out of the wells of salvation. Isaiah 12:1-3

Too often in our modern era we forget that lost sinners are under the anger, and the wrath of God. We, as Christians, also forget that before our salvation, our conversion by the grace of God through faith in Jesus Christ, we were also under the anger, and the wrath of God. But, of course, that was all changed once we received our salvation. Where once we were adversaries now we are friends, where once there was enmity now there is relationship, where once we could only expect wrath now we are given aid and comfort. Yes, God is now not only salvation He is our salvation. He is no longer just the Father of creation, He is our Father and we are His sons and daughters. Being sons and daughters we trust and know that our Father has our best interest at heart. What then are we to be afraid of? Certainly it is not God. Neither can it be man, for, "If God be for us who can be against us?" No longer must we rely on our own strength for now we are inhabited by the strength of the Lord in which all things are possible. Therefore we sing a new song of hope, of praise, and of joy as we draw living water from the well of our salvation. The well of our salvation is, of course, Jesus. Jesus tells us about this well in *John 4:10 & 14.*

Meditation Thirteen

Howl

Howl ye; for the day of the LORD is at hand; it shall come as a destruction from the Almighty. Therefore shall all hands be faint, and every man's heart shall melt: And they shall be afraid: pangs and sorrows shall take hold of them; they shall be in pain as a woman that travaileth: they shall be amazed one at another; their faces shall be as flames. Behold, the day of the LORD cometh, cruel both with wrath and fierce anger, to lay the land desolate: and he shall destroy the sinners thereof out of it. Isaiah 13:6-9

Over the years I've watched numerous apocalyptic movies, probably more than I should have. I've seen the world destroyed by space invaders, natural disasters, and man made holocaust, in all of these the dreadful howls, screams, and wails of the human race on the brink of destruction were a very prevalent part of the annihilation taking place, and so it shall be when the Lord returns with His angels and His saints to rain down destruction on the earth. Evil men's hearts shall turn to wax and melt within them. There will be no solace in the mighty armadas and armies that mankind has built for himself. All the pride and arrogance that has been part of men's psyche shall be turned into the night terrors of a child. The swift onset of fear, pain and sorrow can only be described in the terms of a woman in the last stages of contractions before childbirth. Pain that is unrelenting wracking the body in wave after wave, and then it finally arrives that utter gut wrenching horror as the person beside you bursts into flames. The final day has come, God has had enough, His anger is fierce and His wrath is unrelenting. After millennia of reaching out to a race of beings created in His own image, judgment will come. The days of defiance will now be over as the land is laid desolate and sinners are destroyed.

Meditation Fourteen

A World at Rest

The whole earth is at rest, and is quiet: they break forth into singing. Yea, the fir trees rejoice at thee, and the cedars of Lebanon, saying, Since thou art laid down, no feller is come up against us. Isaiah 14:7 & 8

Stop for a minute and try to think of a time when the whole world was at rest. The eons of time must be peeled back like an artichoke, all the way back to the Garden of Eden. Before Cain murdered Able, before Adam and Eve were cast from the garden, before they succumbed to the temptation of the serpent and rebelled against God. This can be only one time, a time perhaps in the not too distant future. A time known as the Millennial Reign of Christ, a time so feared by a secular world, a time when a Judeo-Christian theocracy shall hold sway over all the earth with Jesus as its head. The global wars under the Antichrist will be over, the mass executions of Christians and Jews will have been abated. So-called natural disasters will have ceased and the intervening hand of God will be stilled. And the world will be at rest. For a moment the world will be encapsulated in silence as the dust settles and the air is stilled, while the curse that the planet has labored under for so long is lifted. And then as if on some cosmic cue the whole earth will break out in singing to the Lamb of God slain for the sins of the world, now the King of Kings and Lord of Lords. Once upon a time, Palestine had great cedar forests. Through ages of war and building programs those forests were laid waste and never replanted. Now the winds sift sand across a wasteland. But during the Millennial Reign of Christ the climate and topography will change, reforestation will take place and a thousand years of green will begin.

Meditation Fifteen

The Cost of Sin

The burden of Moab. Because in the night Ar of Moab is laid waste, and brought to silence; because in the night Kir of Moab is laid waste, and brought to silence… Isaiah 15:1

Your sins shall find you out. No man's an island, tired clichés or so much more? Did you ever wonder how the nation of Moab came to be? Probably not, but its still very important, so sit back and be regaled by the Word of God. Lot escaped from Sodom and Gomorrah with his wife, who turned into a pillar of salt, and his two daughters. In a drunken stupor an incestuous relationship took place where upon both of his daughters became pregnant. The oldest daughter's son was named, you guessed it, Moab, *Genesis 19:30-37.* The ancestors of Lot became enemies of the ancestors of Abraham. Later Lot's ancestors had a king by the name of Balak. This king employed a prophet for hire, named Balaam, to curse the ancestors of Abraham, who are now known as Israel. It has always been interesting to me that Ruth was a Moabitess. She had a son by the name of Obed, with her husband Boaz in the family tree of King David, which is the earthly family tree of Jesus. So King David had relatives in Moab and when he was fleeing from Saul he took his mom and dad there, *I Samuel 22:3 & 4.* Now, King Solomon, David's son, in order to please one of his wives built a temple to Chemos, the false god of the Moabites and also to Molech the false god of the Ammonites, *I Kings 11:7.* But you will remember that Lot had two daughters, the younger one was also pregnant with a son and his name was Ammon. The bane of that sin was still being reaped 800 years later, with the total destruction of Moab by the Assyrians.

Meditation Sixteen

Send the Lamb

Send ye the lamb to the ruler of the land from Sela to the wilderness, unto the mount of the daughter of Zion. Isaiah 16:1

This whole chapter continues with a description of the destruction of Moab. Most of the Moabites have fled from their own country into a city named Sela. Sela is just another name for the rock city of Petra, the capital of Edom. The Moabites supposed that they were safe there in the confines of the wilderness. Isaiah's message to them was the same as it is to you and I. The only true safety is in the recognition of the one true God. How were they to signify that they understood this? They were to take a lamb, have it sent to the King of Judah where it was to be sacrificed in Jerusalem, as they had done in the past. Does any of this sound familiar? *John 1:29 "The next day John seeth Jesus coming unto him, and saith, Behold the Lamb of God, which taketh away the sin of the world."* Was there a good reason that the Moabites should have aligned themselves with the righteous remnant of Judah? All they had to do was believe the word of God that came from the man of God. Because the prophecy had already been given that Judah would not be destroyed by Assyria, it would only be punished, *Isaiah 10:24 & 25 "Therefore thus saith the Lord GOD of hosts, O my people that dwellest in Zion, be not afraid of the Assyrian: he shall smite thee with a rod, and shall lift up his staff against thee, after the manner of Egypt. For yet a very little while, and the indignation shall cease, and mine anger in their destruction.* "But the Moabites had a sin problem; their sin problem was pride. You see, they were a religious people; they just refused to serve the one true God through the sacrifice of the blood of the lamb. Instead they thought they could make it their own way, and so they were lost.

Meditation Seventeen

Respect

At that day shall a man look to his Maker, and his eyes shall have respect to the Holy One of Israel. Isaiah 17:7

Look around you, there are not that many people turning to God, turning to Jesus as maker and creator. Does this cause a conflict in your mind? After all did not God create the heavens and earth as recorded in *Genesis 1:1?* Yes, of course, He did. Jesus who is God, who came in the flesh is the creator, *Hebrews 1:1 & 2 "God, who at sundry times and in divers manners spake in time past unto the fathers by the prophets, Hath in these last days spoken unto us by his Son, whom he hath appointed heir of all things, by whom also he made the worlds;"* Did you catch the last part of verse 2, that it was the Son, Jesus, who made the planets? But, of course, in time of war people do seem to turn to God more often. Even in our society today there is still, if only temporarily, a resurgence of people seeking God after an act of war. Church attendance in the United States spiked 30% after the attacks of September 11, 2001, with people seeking God. Of course, it didn't hold and slipped back 30% after 90 days. The day is coming, however, when all of mankind shall look to his Maker, but not only look to Him but also look at Him. Jesus will finally get His due as, world wide, all eyes turn towards Him in awe and respect for the Holy One of Israel.

Meditation Eighteen

Black Beauty

Woe to the land shadowing with wings, which is beyond the rivers of Ethiopia: Isaiah 18:1

So often the black race is over looked when it comes to expositors of Biblical prophesy. Yet, in the past, present and future they play a very important role. This word woe you must understand can be translated as "ho" as in listen up, or "ah" as ah you're so special. This land south of the Nile Rivers, and there are three, is still referred to as the land of the wings, being noted for its bird population. Ethiopia and Israel have long ties. It is believed that the Queen of Sheba had a son by Solomon, Menelik I. The Emperor of Ethiopia today, Haile Selassie, claims to be the 225th descendant of Menelik I. One of the Pharaohs of Egypt, Necho II, was not Egyptian but Ethiopian, *II Chronicles 35:20-22 "After all this, when Josiah had prepared the temple, Necho king of Egypt came up to fight against Carchemish by Euphrates: and Josiah went out against him. But he sent ambassadors to him, saying, What have I to do with thee, thou king of Judah? I come not against thee this day, but against the house wherewith I have war: for God commanded me to make haste: forbear thee from meddling with God, who is with me, that he destroy thee not. Nevertheless Josiah would not turn his face from him, but disguised himself, that he might fight with him, and hearkened not unto the words of Necho from the mouth of God, and came to fight in the valley of Megiddo.* "And then, of course, we have the story of the Ethiopian eunuch in *Acts 8:26-39.* Today some think the Ark of the Covenant is housed and protected in a bunker at Saint Mary's of Zion Church located at Axum, Ethiopia. When the battle of Armageddon is over all the nations of the world will come to Jerusalem, to Mt. Zion. The Lord wants all the nations to see the ensign on Mt. Zion that will come from Ethiopia. Could this ensign be the lost Ark of the Covenant?

Meditation Nineteen

Back in the Fold

The burden of Egypt. Behold, the LORD rideth upon a swift cloud, and shall come into Egypt: and the idols of Egypt shall be moved at his presence, and the heart of Egypt shall melt in the midst of it. Isaiah 19:1

Historically Egypt started out monotheistic, but soon slid into the morass of idol worship. Today they have returned to monotheism but under the moon god of Islam. But during the millennium, the thousand-year reign of Christ upon the earth, Egypt will once again come into the fold and worship the Lord God. The worship of the Lord will be in a pure language, apparently Hebrew. And although Egypt will retain its own language, five cities will be set aside to worship the Lord, Jesus, in Hebrew. One of the cities will be Heliopolis, the city of destruction or city of the sun. The Egyptians will build a centrally located altar for the worship of the Lord, and on the main highway there shall be a pillar proclaiming that worship. I hate to use a phrase from Robert L. Riply but, "believe it or not," Egypt is one of three nations that will hold a special place in the Lord's heart. The other two are Assyria, and, of course, Israel, all three will receive a special blessing during the millennium. Before this, however, there will be a special judgment against Egypt that will bring them to the Lord in repentance, a repentance that the Lord will forgive. What is this judgment? I'm not sure, but it may be that the Lord uses the Antichrist to smite Egypt for aligning themselves with Russia in the middle of the tribulation period. And finally during the thousand years, a new super highway will be constructed between these three blessed nations, Egypt, Israel, and Assyria.

Meditation Twenty

Getting Naked

And the LORD said, Like as my servant Isaiah hath walked naked and barefoot three years for a sign and wonder upon Egypt and upon Ethiopia; So shall the king of Assyria lead away the Egyptians prisoners, and the Ethiopians captives, young and old, naked and barefoot, even with their buttocks uncovered, to the shame of Egypt. Isaiah 20: 3 & 4

The whole idea here is to show Israel that neither Ethiopia nor Egypt could stand under the might of the Assyrian juggernaut, so there was no sense in trying to make an alliance with them. You will usually find that Egypt in the Bible is a type of the world. Israel was not to align itself with the world. Christian do you think the church should align itself with the world? It's something to think about isn't it? Especially when so many of our leaders in the community are telling us we need to, need to take on the secular culture of the world to evangelize the lost, need to take on unholy alliances to be good stewards of the earth, need to form alliances with pagan countries for military security. Each time we make a compromise we shed a piece of our Christianity, until finally we are naked before the world, perhaps covered only by the loincloth of our salvation.

Most of the commentators will tell you that Isaiah did not really preach naked for three years, that what he actually did was just lay aside his outer garment of mourning, because nudity is so revolting to the people of the Middle East. Perhaps Isaiah did wear a covering for his loins, however, naked is the exact way the Assyrian army took prisoners. Have you been taken naked by Satan in your sins?

Meditation Twenty-One

Looking for Dawn

Therefore are my loins filled with pain: pangs have taken hold upon me, as the pangs of a woman that travaileth: I was bowed down at the hearing of it; I was dismayed at the seeing of it. My heart panted, fearfulness affrighted me: the night of my pleasure hath he turned into fear unto me. The burden of Dumah. He calleth to me out of Seir, Watchman, what of the night? Watchman, what of the night? Isaiah 21: 3, 4, & 11

The atrocities and horrors of war cause us great pain, anguish and sorrow. Yes, we rejoice in the victories over our enemies, yet, to be a witness leaves no one unaffected. These visions literally made Isaiah sick, just as the prophet Daniel's visions made him sick. The prophecies in this chapter appear to cover three very specific time periods, three great battles, three periods of destruction. Two have already transpired, one in 702 B.C. and one in 539 B.C. The third, which is detailed in Revelation 17 and 18, is yet to come. During the time of tribulation and apocalypse, the refugee remnant of Israel will be cared for in the rock city, Petra, in silence so as not to draw attention to them. Dumah is a symbolic word meaning silence. The inquiry came out of Seir, the first man of Seir was Esau and the Kingdom of Esau was Edom, where Petra is. What was the inquiry? How much of the night is left, as the refugees from Israel will be looking for the day, the Son, the return of the Messiah. The watchman will cry out, "the morning cometh." It will come for the Jews who will survive the 7 years of tribulation and wait for the return of the Lord, *Malachi 4:1-5.* For you and I our long dark night will end when the Lord returns in the clouds and calls the church out in the rapture.

Meditation Twenty-Two

Tomorrow We Die

Therefore said I, Look away from me; I will weep bitterly, labour not to comfort me, because of the spoiling of the daughter of my people. And in that day did the Lord GOD of hosts call to weeping, and to mourning, and to baldness, and to girding with sackcloth: And behold joy and gladness, slaying oxen, and killing sheep, eating flesh, and drinking wine: let us eat and drink; for to morrow we shall die. And it was revealed in mine ears by the LORD of hosts, Surely this iniquity shall not be purged from you till ye die, saith the Lord GOD of hosts. Isaiah 22:4, 12-14

God will often push you right to your limit physically, emotionally, and mentally, especially His prophets, preachers, and teachers. That's why I always remind people that Christianity is not for sissies. Isaiah is falling apart. God has pushed him to the breaking point with vision after vision of carnage, war and destruction. He is so distraught that he doesn't even want to be comforted he just wants to cry. All this time God wanted His people to repent, turn from their sin and be truly sorry and humble before Him. And that is what He wants from you and I today. With the mess we're in as a nation, but even more so as His church, we should be prostrate on the floor begging for His forgiveness. And yet, we seem to have the same attitude they did. Eat, drink, and be merry for tomorrow we die, or, you only go around once so grab all the gusto you can. The Lord tells us to "be Holy as He is Holy," His counsel to us is to live temperate, chaste lives of modesty and moderation. But everything about us screams excess and narcissism, greed and avarice. What a burden the prophets of God had to bear then, and what a burden they have to bear today. And then God whispered into the ear of Isaiah, "The only way these people will stop sinning is if they're dead." Have we reached this point of no return?

Meditation Twenty-Three

The Port is Closed

The burden of Tyre. Howl, ye ships of Tarshish; for it is laid waste, so that there is no house, no entering in: from the land of Chittim it is revealed to them. Be still, ye inhabitants of the isle; thou whom the merchants of Zidon, that pass over the sea, have replenished. Isaiah 23:1 & 2

All through history merchant cities on shipping lanes have been great centers of commerce and wealth in the world. Tyre and Zidon were two of those cities during ancient times. They were also cities of great decadence and sin. Nothing much has changed over twenty-five hundred years. Today if you're a merchant marine or a sailor and you're looking for a "good time" and you're in the U.S. you might choose one of our great ports of call, New York in the east, in the northwest Seattle or Portland, Long Beach in the west or in the south perhaps Galveston. Tyre and Zidon had a relation similar to that of England and Hong Kong. We often think that it was Nebuchadnezzar's army that destroyed the costal city of Tyre. Yet, it is the Lord of Hosts who takes full responsibility and credit for it. Egypt you will remember is a type of the world and was greatly pained over the loss of this great port. Can you imagine how the world would bemoan the loss of, say, Seattle or New York? How exacting the Bible is, for seventy years the coastal city would not be allowed to conduct commerce under Babylonian oppression. Then it would be rebuilt only to be destroyed again, this time by Alexander the Great. So, is there any place in the future for Tyre? Is the once great port of call to be forever doomed to stay a fishing village where nets are mended? Yes, it does seem that God has a plan for it in the millennium, where it will become a major distribution point for "J.C. Shipping Lines" of food and clothing to the Middle East. The Lord can take the worst situations and make something good of them.

Meditation Twenty-Four

Isaiah's Apocalypse

Behold, the LORD maketh the earth empty, and maketh it waste, and turneth it upside down, and scattereth abroad the inhabitants thereof. Isaiah 21:1

This chapter is sometimes referred to as Isaiah's apocalypse, the book of Revelation, Revelation means apocalypse. Isaiah, of course, does it in a much more condensed form. Have you ever wondered why the world must go through so much devastation before the utopian society under Jesus can begin? God does give us the reasons for His judgment and purification project. The planet must be cleansed because the people God created to be stewards of it have polluted it so badly. Being a good steward does not make you a tree hugging Giah worshiper it just makes you a good steward. The second reason is that the Laws of God have been transgressed. Thirdly, man has changed the natural ordinances of God, and lastly man has broken God's everlasting covenant. The party for the world will be over and destruction will begin as it continues year after year. The lost of the tribulation will breath a heavy sigh; all they want to do is get drunk and forget their problems. But the four horsemen have been riding through the earth and the grain and the grapes will have all been destroyed. There will be nowhere else to run and no place left to hide. Still through all this those who have been "left behind" and receive Christ as Savior, the remnant from all over the earth, will sing praises to the Lord because they will see His righteous hand in all that will transpire.

Meditation Twenty-Five

Better Days Ahead

O LORD, thou art my God; I will exalt thee, I will praise thy name; for thou hast done wonderful things; thy counsels of old are faithfulness and truth. For thou hast been a strength to the poor, a strength to the needy in his distress, a refuge from the storm, a shadow from the heat, when the blast of the terrible ones is as a storm against the wall. He will swallow up death in victory; and the Lord GOD will wipe away tears from off all faces; and the rebuke of his people shall he take away from off all the earth: for the LORD hath spoken it. Isaiah 25:1, 4 & 8

In Chapter 24 we took a look at the apocalypse through the eyes of Isaiah, in the next three chapters, 25-27, we are going to move into the Kingdom Age or Millennium Reign, if you will. The Kingdom Age is the 1,000 years that Christ reigns on earth. If we are living in the Kingdom Age, and this is our "best life now," God has surely been a disappointment to me, and we should probably re-evaluate the question, "is this all there is?" I believe that all through the Bible it teaches that there are better days ahead. Anyway it's time to do some more thinking and soul searching. So, you have to ask why, after the worldwide destruction, famines, plagues, and disasters of the 7-year tribulation period, will people be exalting and praising God for all the wonderful things He has done? It is because God has kept His word. He will do exactly what He said He would do. He will deliver the Jew and Gentile alike that believe on Him. Now the table will be turned. No longer will it be the strong, the rich, and the mighty that control the wealth and run the world. During the Kingdom Age it will be the weak, humble, poor and needy that will be in charge. For the remnant, as it is for you and I today, death will be swallowed up in victory and God will wipe away all our tears. And finally, finally the Jew will no longer be hated by the nations of the earth. No longer will Christians be ridiculed by the so-called intellectual elite, finally all will be right with the world.

Meditation Twenty-Six

Number One Hit

In that day shall this song be sung in the land of Judah; We have a strong city; salvation will God appoint for walls and bulwarks. Open ye the gates, that the righteous nation which keepeth the truth may enter in. Thou wilt keep him in perfect peace, whose mind is stayed on thee: because he trusteth in thee. Trust ye in the LORD for ever: for in the LORD JEHOVAH is everlasting strength: For he bringeth down them that dwell on high; the lofty city, he layeth it low; he layeth it low, even to the ground; he bringeth it even to the dust. The foot shall tread it down, even the feet of the poor, and the steps of the needy. The way of the just is uprightness: thou, most upright, dost weigh the path of the just. Isaiah 26:1-7

There will be a new number one song in the Israelites top 40, and this is it. The phrase, "in that day" tells us this song will be sung during the Kingdom Age, the Millennium. So just what is it the people of the land of Judah will be singing about? They will be singing about the salvation of God. They will be singing that the salvation of Jesus is like a city with impregnable walls and bulwarks. And when Messiah is ruling in Jerusalem and with it under His protection people from all over the world will be coming on pilgrimage. The gates of Jerusalem will be open wide to all that are keeping or seeking the truth of salvation by grace through faith in Jesus Christ. The way to perfect peace will now be clear, no more searching, no more wondering if you're on the right path. But, of course, that path is open to you and I today. It is keeping our minds centered and focused on Jesus and trusting in Him. The world over, people are looking for everlasting life, eternal health, invulnerability and super strength. All this is available, but can only be found in one place, and it comes by the way of trusting in Jesus. The irony is those that wanted to rule the world, that took advantage of the poor and needy, that closed their hearts and wallets and moved to gated cities, will have their cities destroyed. The disenfranchised, the outcast, the homeless, the so-called trailer trash, the working poor, those who only kept going by trusting in the Lord will now be walking over the destroyed cities that they were not welcome in. If you trust in Jesus you know it is He who holds the scales in the balance. And we are weighed by our faith in Jesus and His righteousness.

Meditation Twenty-Seven

The Two-Edged Sword

In that day the LORD with his sore and great and strong sword shall punish leviathan the piercing serpent, even leviathan that crooked serpent; and he shall slay the dragon that is in the sea. Isaiah 27:1

This is the last of three specific chapters dealing with the Kingdom Age that began in Chapter 25. If you dare to classify yourself as a fundamentalist then you have probably been accused of taking the Bible too literally. So, is there a time when you shouldn't take the Bible literally? Sure there is, when scripture tells you to take it another way. The way to rightly divide the Word of God is to compare scripture with scripture. Let me show you how this works. The phrase "in that day" indicates a period of time from the rapture through the seven years of tribulation all the way to the end of the Kingdom Age, one thousand years. So what is this "great strong sword" the Lord possesses? Part of the answer is found in *Revelation 1:16 "And he had in his right hand seven stars: and out of his mouth went a sharp twoedged sword: and his countenance was as the sun shineth in his strength."* The sword that will punish the old serpent and destroy the Antichrist will come out of the mouth of Jesus and cut both ways. Still we need a little more clarification. Let's look at *Hebrews 4:12 "For the word of God is quick, and powerful, and sharper than any two edged sword, piercing even to the dividing asunder of soul and spirit, and of the joints and marrow, and is a discerner of the thoughts and intents of the heart."* Now we know that the sword of the Lord is the spoken Word of God. Jesus used it to put Satan to flight in the wilderness temptations. Okay, who then is the piercing, crooked serpent? *Revelation 20:2 "And he laid hold on the dragon, that old serpent, which is the Devil, and Satan, and bound him a thousand years,"* this gives us the answer. We end with the destruction of the dragon, the Antichrist that dwells in the sea of humanity.

Meditation Twenty-Eight

Bottle Feeding

Whom shall he teach knowledge? and whom shall he make to understand doctrine? them that are weaned from the milk, and drawn from the breasts. For precept must be upon precept, precept upon precept; line upon line, line upon line; here a little, and there a little: But the word of the LORD was unto them precept upon precept, precept upon precept; line upon line, line upon line; here a little, and there a little; that they might go, and fall backward, and be broken, and snared, and taken. Isaiah 28:9, 10, & 13

Isaiah would really like to share what he has learned from God with his people. So he asks the question, "Who out there can I share this knowledge with? Whom can I teach doctrine to?" The answer then as it is now is, those who are no longer babes in the Lord. Paul had the very same problem with new believers in the church in Corinth, *I Corinthians 3:1 & 2 And I, brethren, could not speak unto you as unto spiritual, but as unto carnal, even as unto babes in Christ I have fed you with milk, and not with meat: for hitherto ye were not able to bear it, neither yet now are ye able."* Also the writer of Hebrews had the same problem, *Hebrews 5:11-14 Of whom we have many things to say, and hard to be uttered, seeing ye are dull of hearing. For when for the time ye ought to be teachers, ye have need that one teach you again which be the first principles of the oracles of God; and are become such as have need of milk, and not of strong meat. For every one that useth milk is unskilful in the word of righteousness: for he is a babe. But strong meat belongeth to them that are of full age, even those who by reason of use have their senses exercised to discern both good and evil."* Are you having the same problem? It seems "the more things change the more they stay the same." Babes in the Lord must be bottle-fed and can only be taught the basic precepts or principles. If you're wondering why so many sermons and teachers sound alike this is why. It seems God's people can't get past the bottle and onto solid food. Have you ever wondered what we would be like if we were that way in the natural. Thirty-five years old with a bottle hanging out of our mouths. So as a good surrogate parent Isaiah was also trying to give them small bites of meat. So how did the people respond to this way of teaching? They actually mocked Isaiah with it. Yet, because they would not hear these truths, they had backslidden, they had been taken in and snared by the enemy, the devil. Look at how these truths apply to the church today. How do they apply to you?

Meditation Twenty-Nine

Lip Service

Wherefore the Lord said, Forasmuch as this people draw near me with their mouth, and with their lips do honour me, but have removed their heart far from me, and their fear toward me is taught by the precept of men: Therefore, behold, I will proceed to do a marvellous work among this people, even a marvellous work and a wonder: for the wisdom of their wise men shall perish, and the understanding of their prudent men shall be hid. Isaiah 29:13 & 14

In Isaiah's day people were just as religious as they are in our own. Today we are going to church, reciting the Lord's Prayer, the Apostles Creed and learning catechism. We have our statements of faith and talk about "what would Jesus do." Yet, we have learned these by rote. Our lips are moving but our hearts are some place else. It has been estimated that up to 75% of the people who go to church are not true Christians. Yes, lots of religion but not much Christ. Here in America 84% of the population claims to be Christian. What a sham, if that were true our prisons would be virtually empty, politicians could be taken at their word, sexually transmitted disease would be eradicated, alcoholism, drug addiction, sexual perversions, violence and all the vices would be so drastically reduced that our society as we see it today would not exist. What is the marvelous work? Well, then as now, God has stripped our so-called wise men, doctors, scientists, our rulers, and politicians, of their wisdom. But there is another aspect to this "marvelous work", and it is found in *I Corinthians 1:18-25 "For the preaching of the cross is to them that perish foolishness; but unto us which are saved it is the power of God. For it is written, I will destroy the wisdom of the wise, and will bring to nothing the understanding of the prudent. Where is the wise? where is the scribe? where is the disputer of this world? hath not God made foolish the wisdom of this world? For after that in the wisdom of God the world by wisdom knew not God, it pleased God by the foolishness of preaching to save them that believe.*

For the Jews require a sign, and the Greeks seek after wisdom: But we preach Christ crucified, unto the Jews a stumblingblock, and unto the Greeks foolishness; But unto them which are called, both Jews and Greeks, Christ the power of God, and the wisdom of God. Because the foolishness of God is wiser than men; and the weakness of God is stronger than men." We know this is part of the "marvelous work" because Paul quotes verse 14 of Isaiah in verse 19 of his letter to the Corinthians.

Meditation Thirty

The Wrong Counsel

Woe to the rebellious children, saith the LORD, that take counsel, but not of me; and that cover with a covering, but not of my spirit, that they may add sin to sin: Which say to the seers, See not; and to the prophets, Prophesy not unto us right things, speak unto us smooth things, prophesy deceits: For thus saith the Lord GOD, the Holy One of Israel; In returning and rest shall ye be saved; in quietness and in confidence shall be your strength: and ye would not. Isaiah 30:1, 10 & 15

Have you ever wondered why as individuals or as a nation we will seek counsel, direction, and guidance from anyone and everyone except God? The answer, of course, is that we are rebellious. God seems to always be the last one we reach out to in either prayer or His Word. We fail to seek diligently the scriptures but will go to the ends of the earth and pay huge sums for earthly advice. We are looking for someone to help in our time of need, trouble or indecision, some comfort and support. We want to do things our way or anyone's way for that matter as long as it doesn't involve God. To involve God would require a dependency on someone other than us. And so we add one more sin to an already very long list, because to know to do the right thing and then not do it is sin. Not only do we not seek God, we don't want to hear from His messengers either. Because a true prophet, pastor, evangelist, or teacher will point you directly to God and unabashedly speak to you the Word of God. Does it seem to you that people don't want to hear the truth? That they would rather hear things that go down smooth; that they would rather be lied to? Are you in that same boat yourself? All the Lord asks is that we return to Him. I know the world and our lives are filled with toil, trials and troubles. Yet, we can only find salvation, quietness, confidence and strength in the Holy One of Israel, Jesus the Christ.

Meditation Thirty-One

Seek the Lord

Woe to them that go down to Egypt for help; and stay on horses, and trust in chariots, because they are many; and in horsemen, because they are very strong; but they look not unto the Holy One of Israel, neither seek the LORD! Yet he also is wise, and will bring evil, and will not call back his words: but will arise against the house of the evildoers, and against the help of them that work iniquity. Now the Egyptians are men, and not God; and their horses flesh, and not spirit. When the LORD shall stretch out his hand, both he that helpeth shall fall, and he that is holpen shall fall down, and they all shall fail together. Isaiah 31:1-3

God warns us over and over again not to go to the world and the things of the world looking for answers or help. Egypt is a representative of the world. We as a people, we as a nation that claims to be Christian are not to depend on our own military strength or the perceived military strength of any nation we might align ourselves with. We are to seek first, last and always deliverance and protection from the Lord. You see there are three sins going on here in these verses, two in the positive and one in the negative. The first is seeking answers from secular society. The second is dependency on military might, and the third is not seeking the wisdom of the Lord. God is wise; He knows what He is doing. If He makes a promise, He keeps a promise. God does not go back on His Word. Why can't we trust and believe that God has our best interest at heart, that if He says He will protect us He will? Is our life one big contradiction? Are we trusting the Lord for our eternal souls but not with our mortal bodies? Isaiah was trying really hard to make a point. There is only one God and if we depend on anything else, whatever it may be, it becomes god in our life and replaces Him. We so often make the mistake thinking that this is a natural battle when the reality is it is a spiritual one. God fights in the Spirit with the Spirit against an unseen, but all too real, foe. And if we align ourselves with a spiritual enemy of God when the enemy falls so will we.

Meditation Thirty-Two

The King

Behold, a king shall reign in righteousness, and princes shall rule in judgment. Isaiah 32:1

Isaiah is once again talking about the Kingdom Age, the millennium. It is a time when the Lord Jesus will rule and reign over the earth in righteousness for a thousand years. *Jeremiah 23:5 & 6* gives us a second view on this. We can see that the King will come from the line of David, that His Kingdom will prosper, and He will render and execute, put into place, justice throughout the entire earth. During those one thousand years the nation of Israel will be at peace with all the nations of the world. One of the titles that the Jews will use for their King is "The Lord Our Righteousness." You and I can use this same title for Jesus today, because His righteousness and His alone makes us righteous before the Father. Hopefully you have wondered who some of the princes are that Jesus will appoint to rule under Him. Without a doubt one of these will be a resurrected, reanimated King David. If you have any doubts about this you can check it out for yourself in *Isaiah 55:3 & 4; Jeremiah 30:9; Ezekiel 34:23 & 24; and Hosea 3:5.* Another one of these princes appears to be Zerubbabel. He is mentioned in *Haggai 2:20-23.* Are there more? At least 12, *Matthew 19:27 & 28,* the eleven apostles, and the twelfth, I'll let you think about that one. So here is the line up for the Kingdom Age, Jesus King of Kings and Lord of Lord's of all the earth and heavens David the price of Israel, Zerubbabel viceroy of Israel, and the twelve apostles governors of Israel, one for each tribe. And what shall this rule look like? Please take the time to end this devotion by reading aloud *Psalm 22 "My God, my God, why hast thou forsaken me? why art thou so far from helping me, and from the words of my roaring? O my God, I cry in the daytime, but thou hearest not; and in the night season, and am not silent. But thou art holy, O thou that inhabitest the praises of Israel. Our fathers trusted in thee: they trusted, and thou didst deliver them. They cried unto thee, and were delivered: they trusted in thee, and were not confounded. But I am a worm, and no man; a reproach of men, and despised of the people. All they that see me laugh me to scorn: they shoot out the lip, they shake the head, saying, He trusted on the LORD that he would deliver him: let him deliver him, seeing he delighted in him. But thou art he that took me out of the womb: thou didst make me hope when I was upon my mother's breasts. I was cast upon thee from the womb: thou art my God from my mother's belly. Be not far from me; for trouble is near; for there is none to help. Many bulls have compassed me: strong bulls of Bashan have beset me round. They gaped upon me with their mouths, as a ravening and a roaring lion. I am poured out like water, and all my bones are out of joint: my heart is like wax; it is melted in the midst of my bowels. My strength is dried up like a potsherd; and my tongue cleaveth to my jaws; and thou hast brought me into the dust of death. For dogs have compassed me: the assembly of the wicked have inclosed me: they pierced my hands and my feet. I may tell all my bones: they look and stare upon me. They part my garments among them, and cast lots upon my vesture. But be not thou far from me, O LORD: O my strength, haste thee to help me. Deliver my soul from the sword; my darling from the power of the dog. Save me from the lion's mouth: for thou hast heard me from the horns of the unicorns. I will declare thy name unto my brethren: in the midst of the congregation will I praise thee. Ye that fear the LORD, praise him; all ye the seed of Jacob, glorify him; and fear him, all ye the seed of Israel. For he hath not despised nor abhorred the affliction of the afflicted; neither hath he hid his face from him; but when he cried unto him, he heard. My praise shall be of thee in the great congregation: I will pay my vows before them that fear him. The meek shall eat and be satisfied: they shall praise the LORD that seek him: your heart shall live for ever. All the ends of the world shall remember and turn unto the LORD: and all the kindreds of the nations shall worship before thee. For the kingdom is the LORD'S: and he is the governor among the nations. All they that be fat upon earth shall eat and worship: all they that go down to the dust shall bow before him: and none can keep alive his own soul. A seed shall serve him; it shall be accounted to the Lord for a generation. They shall come, and shall declare his righteousness unto a people that shall be born, that he hath done this.*

Meditation Thirty-Three

The Wait is Over

O LORD, be gracious unto us; we have waited for thee: be thou their arm every morning, our salvation also in the time of trouble. The LORD is exalted; for he dwelleth on high: he hath filled Zion with judgment and righteousness. And wisdom and knowledge shall be the stability of thy times, and strength of salvation: the fear of the LORD is his treasure. Now will I rise, saith the LORD; now will I be exalted; now will I lift up myself. For the LORD is our judge, the LORD is our lawgiver, the LORD is our king; he will save us. Isaiah 33:2, 5, 6, 10 & 22

We start out in these verses with a prayer that is appropriate for all who believe and are waiting on the glorious return of the Lord, whether Jew or Gentile. But it is also a prayer aimed squarely at the believing remnant going through those seven years we call the tribulation. It is a prayer for the grace of God; it is a prayer for the strength of His mighty arm each morning when we arise. And it is also a prayer for deliverance and salvation as we go through times of trouble. And so the Lord answers our prayer by living and reigning on the throne of our heart. But there is also a physical throne for Jesus, one in heaven where He is exalted and one on Mt. Zion in Israel where He will be exalted. With Him, He brings wisdom and knowledge, and for the first time in the history of the world, there is global stability. Jesus now openly displays His deity, His majesty and His power. He will be the monarch that He is. He will not ascend the throne of David on the whim of a vacillating society or the strength of a military coupe. No, He will ascend in His own might and His own strength. It is an unbelieving world's worst nightmare, Jesus is asserting Himself as the one true God that He is. *For the LORD is our judge, the LORD is our lawgiver, the LORD is our king; he will save us."* And the people said amen and amen.

Meditation Thirty-Four

Getting Indignant

Come near, ye nations, to hear; and hearken, ye people: let the earth hear, and all that is therein; the world, and all things that come forth of it. For the indignation of the LORD is upon all nations, and his fury upon all their armies: he hath utterly destroyed them, he hath delivered them to the slaughter. Their slain also shall be cast out, and their stink shall come up out of their carcases, and the mountains shall be melted with their blood. Isaiah 34:1-3

The call, the warning, which Isaiah sent out, is for all the nations of the world to listen to the prophecies of this book and heed or hearken to them. In other words they need to apply what they have heard. This is very serious stuff. We should not take the Word of God lightly. We should have an awesome, abiding respect for God, a respect that borders on fear and trembling even for the Christian. In the world of a pacifistic, non-intervening God, it seems that we have forgotten that God is sovereign and everything that happens or does not happen, either was caused by or allowed by God. Try to remember that all the world events that take place, and will transpire during the tribulation are for Jesus to come and take His place as King during the millennium. In these verses the Lord is just a little indignant with the nations and armies of the world. The greatest military defeat the world will ever see will take place as God unleashes His fury on those evil men who will swear allegiance to the antichrist, the human embodiment of Satan. Literally hundreds of millions will die on the battlefield. The army of the Lord will totally overrun the armies of Satan. For a thumbnail sketch of these armies look at *Joel 2:11; Revelation 19:11-16 and Revelation 19:19-21,* so many will die that they won't be able to bury them fast enough. God even tells us where this great army will be buried, and that it will take 7 months to do the job. The valley of burial is just east of the Dead Sea. The job of burying the dead will be so great that a city will be constructed at the site to house the workers, *Ezekiel 39:11-16.* And you wonder why reaching the lost is such and urgent task. The countdown has begun and these events could unfold at any time.

Meditation Thirty-Five

Blossom as a Rose

The wilderness and the solitary place shall be glad for them; and the desert shall rejoice, and blossom as the rose. It shall blossom abundantly, and rejoice even with joy and singing: the glory of Lebanon shall be given unto it, the excellency of Carmel and Sharon, they shall see the glory of the LORD, and the excellency of our God. Isaiah 35:1 & 2

In these verses the tribulation in over and God is pouring out His blessing on the earth. Paul says in *Romans 8:22 "For we know that the whole creation groaneth and travaileth in pain together until now."* We don't seem to understand that since the fall into sin by Adam that the whole earth and all of creation has been groaning in pain under the curse. Thorns, weeds, physical pain, work, violence in nature, even the claws and fangs of the animal kingdom are part of the curse. How far it extends is beyond our imagination, as we have no point of reference to compare it with, having always lived in a post Edenic state. However, Satan will be chained, evil men will be destroyed, and the curse will be lifted. When this happens the Middle East along with the rest of the world "blossoms as a rose." Planet earth will be restored to its original pre-fall lush beauty and glory. All the catastrophes that will take place will do their work in changing the topography and atmosphere of the earth. We can only speculate from what the Bible tells us but it appears that the oceans will be more shallow, the mountains not so high and the valleys not so deep. Perhaps a water vapor canopy will be placed around the earth. Weather patterns will no longer be violent, and the oxygen content will be up. Especially blessed will be the Nation of Israel, for now for the first time, the Jews will be fully following Christ and His commandments, and all the blessings given to them will be kicking in and flowing out to the rest of the world, *Deuteronomy 28:1-4 "And it shall come to pass, if thou shalt hearken diligently unto the voice of the LORD thy God, to observe and to do all his commandments which I command thee this day, that the LORD thy God will set thee on high above all nations of the earth: And all these blessings shall come on thee, and overtake thee, if thou shalt hearken unto the voice of the LORD thy God. Blessed shalt thou be in the city, and blessed shalt thou be in the field. Blessed shall be the fruit of thy body, and the fruit of thy ground, and the fruit of thy cattle, the increase of thy kine, and the flocks of thy sheep."*

Meditation Thirty-Six

Reality of the Moment

Now it came to pass in the fourteenth year of king Hezekiah, that Sennacherib king of Assyria came up against all the defenced cities of Judah, and took them. Isaiah 36:1

In this chapter we are going to take a little break from the prophetical and deal with Isaiah's reality of the moment. Of course, prophecy and reality are the same thing. Someone once said that, "prophecy is just history written in advance." But when we are dealing with the things of the moment those things are our reality, because they are happening in our here and now. The events in this chapter are also recorded in *II Kings chapters 18 & 19 and II Chronicles chapters 29 & 30.* The Assyrian army was the super power of its day. Its army was a juggernaut that marched down from the north, you had a choice, you could surrender or be destroyed, and resistance was futile. The Assyrian army practiced blitzkrieg warfare long before Hitler's Germany. This great army was billeted outside the gates of Jerusalem. How many times have you been assailed by the enemy, surrounded by a spiritual enemy that seemed to be unstoppable, one that was unrelenting in its quest to enslave you, or destroy you? Sometimes it may even appear that the enemy is bemused or surprised that you haven't already surrendered. And so before the final onslaught you are taunted, and belittled. Some of the time the enemy may goad you just to see if you have something left up your sleeve, so to speak. You have been threatened and given ultimatums. Perhaps you have been asked to compromise to receive a lesser punishment, this is called terms of surrender. When all seems lost, "never give up, never surrender." Take all the enemy has said, all they have threatened, don't argue or dispute their claims, stay clam, stay quiet and take it to the King.

Meditation Thirty-Seven

Taking it to God

And it came to pass, when king Hezekiah heard it, that he rent his clothes, and covered himself with sackcloth, and went into the house of the LORD. And Isaiah said unto them, Thus shall ye say unto your master, Thus saith the LORD, Be not afraid of the words that thou hast heard, wherewith the servants of the king of Assyria have blasphemed me. Now therefore, O LORD our God, save us from his hand, that all the kingdoms of the earth may know that thou art the LORD, even thou only. Then the angel of the LORD went forth, and smote in the camp of the Assyrians a hundred and fourscore and five thousand: and when they arose early in the morning, behold, they were all dead corpses. Isaiah 37: 1, 6, 20 & 36

What do you do when you receive really bad information? Obviously, it will cause you great distress, just as it did King Hezekiah. But King Hezekiah knew where to go with his problems and the problems of the nation. He took them to the Lord in great humility. He prostrated himself before God seeking His mercy, grace and intervention. He laid it all on the line yet, still recognizing that God is God. Hezekiah knew God would answer his prayer, he just didn't know what the answer would be. But, he was sure that the answer would come through God's prophet Isaiah. And so he gathered up his Cabinet and religious leaders and sent them to Isaiah. The reply to King Hezekiah, from God, through his prophet was, "don't be afraid." Isn't that the same thing that the Lord tells us today? First and foremost don't be afraid. You see our enemies don't seem to understand that when they come against us they are actually coming against the Lord of the universe. The Lord hears every word, every threat and sees every plan. Be reassured Christian, the Lord knows what's going on. I think, all too often, when we pray we forget to ask God to do things to glorify Himself, so that others may see and fear the almighty God. That others might be convicted of sin, that your crisis might bring them to their own crisis and in so doing bring them to Christ. King Hezekiah had his victory over the greatest army of the world, but no bow was bent, no arrow sailed, no lance was thrust and no sword sang its song of death; for the battle belonged to the Lord. The Lord sent His angel of death and in that one night, 185,000 warriors breathed their last breath. God looks after His own.

✓ Meditation Thirty-Eight

Sick to Death

In those days was Hezekiah sick unto death. And Isaiah the prophet the son of Amoz came unto him, and said unto him, Thus saith the LORD, Set thine house in order: for thou shalt die, and not live. Then Hezekiah turned his face toward the wall, and prayed unto the LORD, Go, and say to Hezekiah, Thus saith the LORD, the God of David thy father, I have heard thy prayer, I have seen thy tears: behold, I will add unto thy days fifteen years. Isaiah 38:1, 2 & 5

King Hezekiah was sick, so sick that he believed that he was about to die. He had a boil; perhaps it was a staff infection. Whatever it was, the poison was raging through his body. Things were about to go from bad to worse. It's one thing to be so sick that you think that you're going to die, it's another to have your doctor come in and confirm those fears by telling you to get your house in order because it's confirmed, you are going to die. In this case instead of a doctor it was the prophet of God, even worse because Isaiah had never been wrong. Have you ever had to face a tragedy in your life? If you haven't you will. Perhaps you have even faced death and God has intervened. Did you grow in your relationship with God? Did it prepare you to face some other trail that was coming in your life? God always knows what He is doing and it is always for our good. Try to keep in mind that God is primarily concerned about our salvation, our relationship to Him, and our spiritual growth. The rest is just window dressing. Hezekiah was so sick he couldn't get out of bed. He most certainly was unable to make it to the temple. The best he could do was just roll over, face the wall, pray and cry. Never think that God doesn't hear your prayer. God may be waiting to show you a miracle. That miracle may be instantaneous or it may take time. It may come through medical means of divine intervention. However, it comes remember it is from God and to give Him the glory.

Meditation Thirty-Nine

Being Stupid

At that time Merodachbaladan, the son of Baladan, king of Babylon, sent letters and a present to Hezekiah: for he had heard that he had been sick, and was recovered. And Hezekiah was glad of them, and shewed them the house of his precious things, the silver, and the gold, and the spices, and the precious ointment, and all the house of his armour, and all that was found in his treasures: there was nothing in his house, nor in all his dominion, that Hezekiah shewed them not. Behold, the days come, that all that is in thine house, and that which thy fathers have laid up in store until this day, shall be carried to Babylon: nothing shall be left, saith the LORD. Then said Hezekiah to Isaiah, Good is the word of the LORD which thou hast spoken. He said moreover, For there shall be peace and truth in my days. Isaiah 39:1, 2, 6 & 8

If you know anything about history you have heard of the Trojan horse. We have a saying that is derived from that incident, it goes like this, "beware of Greeks baring gifts." In this case we could say, "beware of Babylonians baring gifts." Why is our story so important? Because, sometimes our enemy is disguised as our friend, sometimes after a miracle or two, or in Hezekiah's case three, we get so excited about what God has done, we let our guard down and become complacent and stupid. Often times the enemy of our faith does not do an immediate, frontal attack. Sometimes it is the second or third generation that will pay for our folly. Sometimes we are living in the moment so much that we don't consider the possible consequences in the future. Yes, we are to be gentle as doves but we are also to be wise as serpents. God living in the future as much as the present and past sees the impact of our indiscretions as far out as they go. Sometimes we just make mistakes, when we do and they are brought to our attention, let us humble ourselves before God for He is righteous and Holy. The next thing that we need to do is recognize that God is gracious and merciful, and sometimes we don't have to face the consequences of our poor decisions. How gracious and merciful is God? If you have been saved you know, because you no longer have to face the eternal consequences of your sin.

Meditation Forty

The Voice

The voice of him that crieth in the wilderness, Prepare ye the way of the LORD, make straight in the desert a highway for our God. The grass withereth, the flower fadeth: but the word of our God shall stand for ever. To whom then will ye liken me, or shall I be equal? saith the Holy One. But they that wait upon the LORD shall renew their strength; they shall mount up with wings as eagles; they shall run, and not be weary; and they shall walk, and not faint. Isaiah 40:3, 8, 25 & 31

That verse three applies to John the Baptist is without question, for all four Gospels record it this way. That this verse applies to the spiritual condition of people's hearts is also without question. The heart without God, without Jesus, is like a desert, a dry barren wasteland. For it to be changed to an oasis alive and springing up with water there must be a direct pathway built on it straight to God and that pathway is paved with the blood of Jesus. Every created thing in creation is affected by decay, they weather, they fade, they tarnish, but the Word of God that was made flesh will stand forever. And the embodiment of the Word is Jesus the Christ, everlasting to everlasting the alpha and omega. When we think about God and the personages of the Trinity, Father, Son and Holy Ghost, we are given the rhetorical question, "whom can we compare God to and to whom is He equal?" The answer to this, of course, is no one. We only have the faintest grasp of God, how then could we dare to even attempt to compare Him to anyone else. The most glorious angels in heaven stand before Him in humility with their wings covering their faces and feet as they cry out holy, holy, holy. And yet, as believers, as those who call Him Savior and Lord we are to share in His strength and power, as we renew it in Him, as we come before the Father, cleansed by the blood of the Son and empowered by the Spirit. So let us wait upon the Lord, to be His good and faithful servants, honoring Him with our stewardship of all He has given us, but especially with the Gospel of His Son, Jesus.

Meditation Forty-One

Holding Our Hand

Keep silence before me, O islands; and let the people renew their strength: let them come near; then let them speak: let us come near together to judgment. Fear thou not; for I am with thee: be not dismayed; for I am thy God: I will strengthen thee; yea, I will help thee; yea, I will uphold thee with the right hand of my righteousness. For I the LORD thy God will hold thy right hand, saying unto thee, Fear not; I will help thee. Isaiah 41:1, 10, 13

When dealing with truth we must always be cognizant to rightly divide it. We must remember that certain promises were given only to the nation Israel, while others are spiritual in nature and can be applied to all believers through all the ages. As God's judgment comes upon the earth there is no argument we can make for ourselves so we are to keep silent. The word islands is interesting in that it can have three meanings and should be understood in context; it can simply mean islands, or it can mean seacoasts, finally, it can mean peoples or nations that live the farthest away from Israel. After all, as far as God is concerned Jerusalem is the center of the planet. We are now presented with an invitation to come near to God in silence. My wife and I have been married over three decades and often times we are at our closest when we are simply silent in each other's presence. For a relationship to grow there must be times of quiet and simple awareness so we can grow closer and so it is in our relationship with God. In our quiet and stillness we are better able to recognize the working of the Holy Spirit in our lives, our true strength. In recognizing the strength of God and His righteousness dwelling in us, we become less anxious with the things of life and fear begins to dissipate. We can allow our fears to simply slip away because God is holding our hand and whispering into our hearts, "Fear not, I will help thee."

Meditation Forty-Two

Behold My Servant

Behold my servant, whom I uphold; mine elect, in whom my soul delighteth; I have put my spirit upon him: he shall bring forth judgment to the Gentiles. He shall not cry, nor lift up, nor cause his voice to be heard in the street. A bruised reed shall he not break, and the smoking flax shall he not quench: he shall bring forth judgment unto truth. He shall not fail nor be discouraged, till he have set judgment in the earth: and the isles shall wait for his law. Isaiah 42:1-4

To understand the Old Testament it must be taken in concert with the New Testament. To be secure in the promises of God we must see how they are fulfilled in the New Testament. So let's evaluate this Old Testament prophecy. "Behold my servant," now that brings us to a question, who is Isaiah talking about? Actually we have several options. It could be that Isaiah was speaking of himself, the nation Israel is also referred to as "my servant." The Godly remnant is called "my servant," King Cyrus of Babylon was called "my servant," and of course, the Messiah, Jesus, is called "my servant." How can we know for sure then who this prophesy if referring to? By allowing scripture to interpret scripture, *Matthew 12:15-21 But when Jesus knew it, he withdrew himself from thence: and great multitudes followed him, and he healed them all; And charged them that they should not make him known: That it might be fulfilled which was spoken by Esaias the prophet, saying, Behold my servant, whom I have chosen; my beloved, in whom my soul is well pleased: I will put my spirit upon him, and he shall shew judgment to the Gentiles. He shall not strive, nor cry; neither shall any man hear his voice in the streets. A bruised reed shall he not break, and smoking flax shall he not quench, till he send forth judgment unto victory. And in his name shall the Gentiles trust."* And so now we know; it's all about Jesus: Jesus the Son would be upheld by God the Father, Jesus would be the chosen one, the elect of God, Jesus would judge the

Gentiles as well as the Jews, Jesus would not be a showman, Jesus would come in gentleness and love, Jesus' plan would come about, every nation would hear the plan of salvation

Meditation Forty-Three

Bullet Proof

When thou passest through the waters, I will be with thee; and through the rivers, they shall not overflow thee: when thou walkest through the fire, thou shalt not be burned; neither shall the flame kindle upon thee. Even every one that is called by my name: for I have created him for my glory, I have formed him; yea, I have made him. Isaiah 43:2 & 7

Here we see God's promise to be with the remnant of Israel through all their troubles. There are allusions here to both the past and the future, the crossing of the Red Sea, the crossing of the Jordan River and being with Shadrack, Meshack, and Abendigo as they were cast into the fiery furnace. The promise, of course, is not that He would keep them out of trouble but that He would go through it with them. But these promises also apply to all of God's people generally and are great encouraging words to us today. With the promise, however, comes an obligation, the obligation is that we glorify the Lord. If we are to be called by His name then we have been created, formed and made by Him for that very purpose. For me probably the saddest thing in the world is for someone to call himself or herself a Christian and not glorify Christ. These verses are just like reading the New Testament. The Lord has chosen us we have not chosen Him. We have been chosen that we might know God, that we might believe God, and understand that He is the one and only God. That there is no other God before God and there is no other God after God, there is only God. How privileged is that? But with that privilege comes the responsibility to do something and that something is to witness of Him and for Him, because there is no other Savior outside the Lord God, Jesus the Christ.

Meditation Forty-Four

Looking for Directions

For I will pour water upon him that is thirsty, and floods upon the dry ground: I will pour my spirit upon thy seed, and my blessing upon thine offspring: I have blotted out, as a thick cloud, thy transgressions, and, as a cloud, thy sins: return unto me; for I have redeemed thee. Thus saith the LORD, thy redeemer, and he that formed thee from the womb, I am the LORD that maketh all things; that stretcheth forth the heavens alone; that spreadeth abroad the earth by myself... Isaiah 44:3, 22 & 24

The human soul is dry and barren, separated from God, the source of living water by sin. Perhaps you are aware of the encounter Jesus had with the woman at the well. She was desolate, broken, bitter and argumentative. For her to flower she would need this living water. Look at the offer that only God can make, *John 4: 10, 13 & 14 "Jesus answered and said unto her, If thou knewest the gift of God, and who it is that saith to thee, Give me to drink; thou wouldest have asked of him, and he would have given thee living water. Jesus answered and said unto her, Whosoever drinketh of this water shall thirst again: But whosoever drinketh of the water that I shall give him shall never thirst; but the water that I shall give him shall be in him a well of water springing up into everlasting life."* The way to receive this living water then is by grace, through faith in Jesus Christ. Our sins are not only described as a dry desert but as a thick cloud as well. If you've ever been on a mountain surrounded by clouds or ever flew through a bank of them in an aircraft, you've probably noticed that you quickly become disoriented, not knowing up from down or being able to see where you've been or where you're going. So as a child of God, one of those who have been redeemed, those clouds have been removed from your life. You can now determine what is right or wrong, and up from down. You can now see were you've been and where you're going. No longer is your vision, your life obscured by the clouds of sin, not only is this for the lost, it is also for those who have wandered back into some of those clouds. Now you have been implanted with a homing device, the Holy Spirit and He will lead you out of those clouds if you will follow Him and go in the direction He is pointing. The Lord confirms all this by re-asserting Himself as creator of you and I from the time of our conception, and as creator of all other things that He stretched out from the singularity of His mind.

Meditation Forty-Five

Pots and Clay

Woe unto him that striveth with his Maker! Let the potsherd strive with the potsherds of the earth. Shall the clay say to him that fashioneth it, What makest thou? or thy work, He hath no hands? Woe unto him that saith unto his father, What begettest thou? or to the woman, What hast thou brought forth? For thus saith the LORD that created the heavens; God himself that formed the earth and made it; he hath established it, he created it not in vain, he formed it to be inhabited: I am the LORD; and there is none else. Look unto me, and be ye saved, all the ends of the earth: for I am God, and there is none else. Isaiah 45:9, 10, 18 & 22

When your father gives you a warning it is a good idea to listen to that warning. When God the Father gives you the warning you had better listen. And yet, we live in a country of sniveling, whining people. Even worse we live in a country of sniveling, whining Christians. The warning to us is to stop complaining, arguing and fighting with God. You will not win! Now, you might get away with it with another person but you don't have a chance with God. Put yourself in this analogy, as the potter you just put a lump of clay on the turntable and started working it into a pot or bowl. You would not expect that piece of clay to start complaining to you about how it was being made or what job it would perform, whether it would be a flower pot, a water pot or a human waste pot. The clay does not make itself nor can it complain about another pot. Just as a child has no right to complain about being born, neither were they able to have anything to do with it, or even with how they came out looking. Neither do we have a right to contend with God on this issue. God reasserts His sovereign authority by reminding us that it was He who created the atmospheric heaven that we breathe. It was He that created the stellar heavens that contain all the stars and planets. It was He that created the celestial heaven where He and His legions dwell.

He created the earth, made it and formed it. He established the earth for a reason, so it could be inhabited. In so doing He established Himself as the one and only God. And in so doing we have only one person to look to, to be saved, from all the ends of the earth there is only one God. And He became flesh and dwelt with us. His name is Jesus.

Meditation Forty-Six

Looked After

Hearken unto me, O house of Jacob, and all the remnant of the house of Israel, which are borne by me from the belly, which are carried from the womb: And even to your old age I am he; and even to hoar hairs will I carry you: I have made, and I will bear; even I will carry, and will deliver you. Remember the former things of old: for I am God, and there is none else; I am God, and there is none like me, Declaring the end from the beginning, and from ancient times the things that are not yet done, saying, My counsel shall stand, and I will do all my pleasure: Isaiah 46:3, 4, 9 & 10

These are such comforting words. Words that will help you understand just how special you are. Listen, it is God who conceived you in the womb, and God who looked after you in the womb to deliver you. I know some of you are hurting and broken, you would say, "but I'm a product of rape or incest." Perhaps you were never loved or wanted by your parents, some of you are dealing with the side affects of being a baby born to an addict or alcoholic. I can't give you all the answers that you want to all the why's you have. But I've lived long enough and gone through enough tragedies in my own life to assure you that if you will let Him, God can take the worse case scenario and make something good of it. You see from the moment of conception God knows His people. And all through their lives, from babies to toddlers, from toddlers to teenagers, from teenagers to middle age and from middle age to seniors God knows us, He created us, He cares for us, He watches over us, He delivers us, He saves us and He keeps us. To help us get through, God tells us to remember all the things He has done in the past. Remember the lives and miracles recorded from Genesis through Revelation. Remember all the prophecies and all that have come true. Remember that He proclaims what the end will be from the beginning. Remember His Word will stand for time and eternity, and that all He said He would do, He will do. And when you're done with all that trace back through the memories of your own life, the good and the bad. Look at where you were and see how far you've come. The future is only uncertain from our point of view. Be assured there is a glorious end for the remnant that believes.

Meditation Forty-Seven

The Dark Side

But these two things shall come to thee in a moment in one day, the loss of children, and widowhood: they shall come upon thee in their perfection for the multitude of thy sorceries, and for the great abundance of thine enchantments. For thou hast trusted in thy wickedness: thou hast said, None seeth me. Thy wisdom and thy knowledge, it hath perverted thee; and thou hast said in thine heart, I am, and none else beside me. Stand now with thine enchantments, and with the multitude of thy sorceries, wherein thou hast laboured from thy youth; if so be thou shalt be able to profit, if so be thou mayest prevail. Thou art wearied in the multitude of thy counsels. Let now the astrologers, the stargazers, the monthly prognosticators, stand up, and save thee from these things that shall come upon thee. Isaiah 47:9, 10, 12, & 13

God is so mysterious it's no wonder we can't figure Him out, "His ways are not our ways." God was going to use Babylon to discipline His people. The prophets understood that the nation needed to be disciplined. They just didn't understand why God was going to use an evil, wicked nation like Babylon. But God knew what He was doing, just as He knows what He is doing today. He also wanted the people to know that Babylon was going to get theirs, and why. It was because of sorcery. It's interesting that there has been such resurgence in the mystic arts. Once again they are in *Vogue*, and *Chick*, they are the biggest draw in the literary and movie industry. Add to that the number of games, toys, TV shows, and cultic religions and you can see how quickly we are becoming a nation of spiritists. And this is the reason God destroyed Babylon. Is our day coming? Babylon was also a repository for wisdom, knowledge and secret societies, along with the greatest military the world had ever seen until that time. They also had the greatest minds in the world and because of all this they thought they were invincible. Did you ever wonder where we get our sarcasm from? Of course, ours is perverted, but God is being very sarcastic. If this was written in 21st century English it might sound something like this, "Go ahead get your sorcerers together, do your enchantments, let's see what you've got. Make My day. Come on now, you've been practicing this stuff all your life. Get everybody together, let's see if you can stop this from happening." Christian, be very careful what you dabble in.

Meditation Forty-Eight

Advance Notice

I have declared the former things from the beginning; and they went forth out of my mouth, and I shewed them; I did them suddenly, and they came to pass. Because I knew that thou art obstinate, and thy neck is an iron sinew, and thy brow brass; O that thou hadst hearkened to my commandments! then had thy peace been as a river, and thy righteousness as the waves of the sea: There is no peace, saith the LORD, unto the wicked. Isaiah 48:3, 4, 18 & 22

The prophet Isaiah lays out the pertinent facts. Why did God have to declare things so far in advance? Because He knew His people and they were an obstinate bunch. Obstinate is defined by Merriam - Webster's Collegiate Dictionary 10th edition as "firmly and often perversely adhering to one's purpose or opinion, not yielding to argument, persuasion or pleading." They had necks like iron; you just couldn't turn them in the right direction. And they had heads like solid brass. Does this sound familiar? Do you know any Christians like that? Have you looked in the mirror lately? God let them know things so far in advance because if He had not, they would have given the credit for their deliverance to some stupid idol. How often have you and I given credit to something or someone else besides God? If God's people would only listen to His commandments, things would have been so different. Today if we would only listen to what God's Word is teaching and then follow Him as He leads us in paths of righteousness, if they had only done these things, if we would only do these things, then we would have peace and uninterrupted fellowship with Him. But what of those who will not follow God? They will never have peace whether Jew or Gentile, whether in this world or the next, torment can only be theirs.

Meditation Forty-Nine

Jesus Revealed

Listen, O isles, unto me; and hearken, ye people, from far; The LORD hath called me from the womb; from the bowels of my mother hath he made mention of my name. And he hath made my mouth like a sharp sword; in the shadow of his hand hath he hid me, and made me a polished shaft; in his quiver hath he hid me; And now, saith the LORD that formed me from the womb to be his servant, to bring Jacob again to him, Though Israel be not gathered, yet shall I be glorious in the eyes of the LORD, and my God shall be my strength. And he said, It is a light thing that thou shouldest be my servant to raise up the tribes of Jacob, and to restore the preserved of Israel: I will also give thee for a light to the Gentiles, that thou mayest be my salvation unto the end of the earth. Thus saith the LORD, the Redeemer of Israel, and his Holy One, to him whom man despiseth, to him whom the nation abhorreth, to a servant of rulers, Kings shall see and arise, princes also shall worship, because of the LORD that is faithful, and the Holy One of Israel, and he shall choose thee. Isaiah 49:1, 2, 5, 6 & 7

This is the first of chapters 49-53 that are what I refer to as the anatomy of the Savior. Starting here with the bare bones, no pun intended, each chapter will reveal a little more of Christ to us. When we reach Chapter 53 a very clear picture of Jesus will be revealed to us. The same picture the Jews had of Jesus when God walked among men. From the onset, the Lord called out to the Jews but not only the Jews, all the nations of the world. He wants all to listen to Him and pay attention. He will give us the name of His Son, the Holy One of Israel from His mother's womb, "and thou shalt call His name Jesus." When Jesus spoke, the Word of God came out of His mouth like a sharp sword, which even His enemies would recognize, for, "never man spake like this man." Those sharp words would continue not only the first time He came upon the earth, but will continue with Him to His next return. And not only a sword, but a polished shaft, a dart, that could be launched at a person's heart through the preaching of His Gospel, "Now when they heard this they were pricked in their heart." God would come to earth as the man Jesus, and Jesus' ministry would be primarily to His people the Jews, to call them to Himself, but they would have none of it. Yet, even in that He would be glorified in His Father. And so the ministry of Jesus, the Salvation He offered, would be expanded becoming the light of the Gentile world as well, and reaching to the ends of the earth, as He chose out His from all the people of the world. Jesus was and is hated not only by the Jews but by all the nations of the earth as well. But one day all the world shall bow and worship before the Holy One of Israel, *Philippians 2: 9-11 "Wherefore God also hath highly exalted him, and given him a name which is above every name: That at the name of Jesus every knee should bow, of things in heaven, and things in earth, and things under the earth, And that every tongue should confess that Jesus Christ is Lord, to the glory of God the Father."*

Meditation Fifty

Wisdom and Submission

The Lord GOD hath given me the tongue of the learned, that I should know how to speak a word in season to him that is weary: he wakeneth morning by morning, he wakeneth mine ear to hear as the learned. The Lord GOD hath opened mine ear, and I was not rebellious, neither turned away back. I gave my back to the smiters, and my cheeks to them that plucked off the hair: I hid not my face from shame and spitting. For the Lord GOD will help me; therefore shall I not be confounded: therefore have I set my face like a flint, and I know that I shall not be ashamed. Isaiah 50:4-7

This is the second of chapters 49-53 that I refer to as the anatomy of the Savior: Jesus is speaking in these verses telling what His Father has given Him. The tongue of the learned, *Matthew 13:54 "And when he was come into his own country, he taught them in their synagogue, insomuch that they were astonished, and said, Whence hath this man this wisdom, and these mighty works?"* A word to the weary and downtrodden, *Matthew 11:28 "Come unto me, all ye that labour and are heavy laden, and I will give you rest."* He was open to the teachings of His Father, *Luke 2:46 & 47 "And it came to pass, that after three days they found him in the temple, sitting in the midst of the doctors, both hearing them, and asking them questions. And all that heard him were astonished at his understanding and answers."* Jesus was a carpenter by trade, but as the Son of God He was a student of the Word. Jesus is the only one who could say in all honesty that He did not need to attend church. But He did! On the Sabbath you would find Him there in the temple. Jesus listened to His Father, was never rebellious, and worked at the task He had been given, the one He had volunteered for, *Hebrew 10: 4, 7, 9 & 10 "For it is not possible that the blood of bulls and of goats should take away sins. Then said I, Lo, I come (in the volume of the book it is written of me,) to do thy will, O God. Then said he, Lo, I come to do thy will, O God. He taketh away the first, that he may establish the second. By the which will we are sanctified through the offering of the body of Jesus Christ once for all."* We need only to read the Passion in the Gospels to understand the suffering our Lord endured for us, yet, Jesus was determined to be about the Father's will so that we can have life eternal. Jesus felt the price was worth it all. Thank you!

Meditation Fifty-One

Restoration and Righteousness

For the LORD shall comfort Zion: he will comfort all her waste places; and he will make her wilderness like Eden, and her desert like the garden of the LORD; joy and gladness shall be found therein, thanksgiving, and the voice of melody. Hearken unto me, my people; and give ear unto me, O my nation: for a law shall proceed from me, and I will make my judgment to rest for a light of the people. My righteousness is near; my salvation is gone forth, and mine arms shall judge the people; the isles shall wait upon me, and on mine arm shall they trust. Isaiah 51:3-5

This is the third of the five chapters, Chapters 49-53 that I refer to as the anatomy of the Savior. God has chosen to bless all nations through the seed of Abraham. The primary part of this blessing is, of course, Jesus, as the light to the Gentiles, that's you and I. But another part of that blessing is the restoration of Israel, not only the nation, but also the land itself. Jesus does three things for the Jews, one He comforts Zion. Comfort means different things to different people, to some it is a shoulder to cry on, and with others it might be a leather recliner, an old dress or a pair of tennis shoes. The comfort of Jesus is fit for all His people. The comfort of Israel, by the Lord, will be shared by the Jews with all the nations of the world. Second, the land will be restored to its original condition just like the Garden of Eden. Thirdly, the Jews will be restored as the happiest people in the world, breaking out in spontaneous songs of thanksgiving and joy. Jesus, of course, was the fulfillment of the law and the prophets. The judgment of Jesus is always just and righteous, and it becomes the light of His people and the world. Along with the three restorations we have the triumvirate of righteousness. For the righteousness of God is Jesus, *Romans 10:4 "For Christ is the end of the law for righteousness to every one that believeth."* And the judgment of God is Jesus, *Revelation 19:11 & 15 And I saw heaven opened, and behold a white horse; and he that sat upon him was called Faithful and True, and in righteousness he doth judge and make war. And out of his mouth goeth a sharp sword, that with it he should smite the nations: and he shall rule them with a rod of iron: and he treadeth the winepress of the fierceness and wrath of Almighty God.*

Meditation Fifty-Two

The Marred Visage

Behold, my servant shall deal prudently, he shall be exalted and extolled, and be very high. As many were astonied at thee; his visage was so marred more than any man, and his form more than the sons of men: So shall he sprinkle many nations; the kings shall shut their mouths at him: for that which had not been told them shall they see; and that which they had not heard shall they consider. Isaiah 52:13-15

This is the fourth of Chapters 49-53 that I refer to as the anatomy of the Savior. Jesus always deals wisely, justly and, righteously in Old Testament times and today. Being limited in our scope, able only to live in the present, we often fail to correctly interpret the interventions of Christ in our lives. When Christ returns to rule and reign from Mt. Zion in Jerusalem, He *will* receive the homage, respect, and adulation from the human race that is due Him, due Him for what He did at Calvary. Many were astonished at the appearance of Christ on the cross. You and I cannot visualize how horrible the cross was. Even with the capital punishment of a Roman crucifixion it was not the norm to beat a man's face, rip his back, pull out his beard, and pierce his head with a crown of thorns. Our Lord was a gruesome and hideous sight to behold with only a mass of quivering flesh hanging on the cross, shrouded with an unimaginable covering of grief and sorrow. Take a walk down the street of almost any city and you will find people's faces etched with the sins of their lives. How the countenance of our Lord must have changed as He bore the sins of the world. His blood flowed that day: His blood would be sprinkled on the hearts of people from all nations cleansing us from all sin, making us holy and pure before a righteous God. What will the people of the earth see, hear, and consider as they stand in silence before the King of Kings? *Zechariah 12:10 And I will pour upon the house of David, and upon the inhabitants of Jerusalem, the spirit of grace and of supplications: and they shall look upon me whom they have pierced, and they shall mourn for him, as one mourneth for his only son, and shall be in bitterness for him, as one that is in bitterness for his firstborn." and Zechariah 13:6 "And one shall say unto him, What are these wounds in thine hands? Then he shall answer, Those with which I was wounded in the house of my friends."*

Meditation Fifty-Three

The Total Price

Yet it pleased the LORD to bruise him; he hath put him to grief: when thou shalt make his soul an offering for sin, he shall see his seed, he shall prolong his days, and the pleasure of the LORD shall prosper in his hand. He shall see of the travail of his soul, and shall be satisfied: by his knowledge shall my righteous servant justify many; for he shall bear their iniquities. Therefore will I divide him a portion with the great, and he shall divide the spoil with the strong; because he hath poured out his soul unto death: and he was numbered with the transgressors; and he bare the sin of many, and made intercession for the transgressors. Isaiah 53:10-12

This is the last of the five chapters, Chapters 49-53 that I have referred to as the anatomy of the Savior. Why was God pleased? Pleased means that He was obligated, but why was the Father obligated to offer up His own Son for you and I? Because it was the only way, nothing else was perfect enough, nothing else in all the universe had enough value to the Father to redeem your soul and mine. This is why we should never trivialize the sacrifice of Jesus. Often times we will trivialize His sacrifice simply out of our own ignorance. Some are misinformed or naive and believe that good works or so-called sacraments add a portion of grace to our lives. Don't get me wrong every believer should have good works in their lives. And every believer should follow in the two ordnances that Jesus set before us. But the only grace and all grace come from the Father through faith in the Son. That is why we should never trivialize the sacrifice of Jesus. Because when the Father looked at the travail, the suffering, of His one and only Son upon the cross of Calvary, His holy justice, His holy righteousness, His holy wrath toward the sin of mankind had been satisfied. That is why Jesus said it is finished. All that could be done was done, and it is through the knowledge of Jesus, faith in Him for the forgiveness of our sins that we are justified before God. Jesus took on hell for Himself so that we could take on heaven. Jesus poured out His soul to forgive you and I. Christ is so boldly portrayed in this chapter it is hard for me to understand how any good Jew of the day could mistake Jesus for any other person than the Messiah. Please take the time to read and meditate on this entire chapter then let your heart be moved by the 22nd Psalm.

Meditation Fifty-Four

Heritage of Servants

For thy Maker is thine husband; the LORD of hosts is his name; and thy Redeemer the Holy One of Israel; The God of the whole earth shall he be called. In a little wrath I hid my face from thee for a moment; but with everlasting kindness will I have mercy on thee, saith the LORD thy Redeemer. And all thy children shall be taught of the LORD; and great shall be the peace of thy children. No weapon that is formed against thee shall prosper; and every tongue that shall rise against thee in judgment thou shalt condemn. This is the heritage of the servants of the LORD, and their righteousness is of me, saith the LORD. Isaiah 54: 5, 8, 13 & 17

In these verses the tribulation is over and Jesus has returned to earth. The Jewish remnant, the believing Jews are returning to Israel. The Christian remnant is giving them the number one priority on the few remaining modes of transportation that are still left running. The Maker, the Creator is no longer estranged from His people. Once again, He is their husband as He is the husband to the church. With the Antichrist destroyed and Satan chained in hell for a thousand years, Jesus is truly God of the whole earth. We do not know how many of the Jews accepted the Antichrist as god; perhaps it was as many as two thirds. For a moment Jesus will have to turn away from His earthly race, His earthly heritage, as the wrath of God is rained down upon them, securing only a few under the protection of Michael the Archangel in the fortress called Petra. But all that is past now in these verses, and Jesus reaches out with eternal kindness, that shall never again be withdrawn. And what of the heritage of the few who remain, what of their children? Finally there will be a perfect education system in the world. Jesus, Himself will be teaching at the Synagogue School. The two required courses will be on love and peace. No longer will there be fear of school shootings, stabbings, rape, drugs, gangs or any of the other things that plague our school system today.

Evolution will soon be a forgotten memory with the Creator teaching the origins of man. And the only peer pressure will be to be like Jesus, and their peace will be a thousand years. During the Millennium you will not want to use "hate speech" against a Jew or a Gentile believer. No weapons formed against us will succeed because our righteousness is of the Lord.

Meditation Fifty-Five

A Fat Soul

Ho, every one that thirsteth, come ye to the waters, and he that hath no money; come ye, buy, and eat; yea, come, buy wine and milk without money and without price. Wherefore do ye spend money for that which is not bread? and your labour for that which satisfieth not? hearken diligently unto me, and eat ye that which is good, and let your soul delight itself in fatness. Isaiah 55:1 & 2

Stop and think about the offer of salvation. What Jesus has to offer cannot be bought. I suppose that's why so many poor people come to Jesus. Because our Savior has already paid the price for it with the only currency accepted, Himself. Three refreshing drinks are offered for the thirsty soul, spiritual water, it refreshes, quenches the thirst and hydrates the soul the same way natural water hydrates the body, *John 7:37 & 38 In the last day, that great day of the feast, Jesus stood and cried, saying, If any man thirst, let him come unto me, and drink. He that believeth on me, as the scripture hath said, out of his belly shall flow rivers of living water.* Spiritual wine, drunkenness is certainly frowned on by God and abstinence is encouraged, except when it comes to spiritual wine. With spiritual wine we are allowed, and even encouraged to be drunk. The wine of the Spirit fills us with joy and removes our inhibitions to live a Christian life, *Ephesians 5:18 "And be not drunk with wine, wherein is excess; but be filled with the Spirit;"* Then there is spiritual milk, milk is for growth, it provides strong bones, and teeth for baby Christians. It gives a platform, a frame for which the meat of the Word can build on. We may not like fat bodies, but God sure likes fat souls. He even encourages us to work at putting on those spiritual pounds. So put down the burger and fries and pick up your Bibles. But don't wait too long the Lord is calling the human race to the banquet, and if you don't RSVP you may lose out on your invitation. You might ask yourself how many chances does God have to give you? How many times do you have to refuse before God stops calling? The way to salvation has never changed. We are to come to the Lord, forsake our wicked ways and He will pardon us from our sins.

Meditation Fifty-Six

Keep On Keeping On

Thus saith the LORD, Keep ye judgment, and do justice: for my salvation is near to come, and my righteousness to be revealed. Blessed is the man that doeth this, and the son of man that layeth hold on it; that keepeth the sabbath from polluting it, and keepeth his hand from doing any evil. Even them will I bring to my holy mountain, and make them joyful in my house of prayer: Isaiah 55:1 & 2, & 7 a & b

Do you ever get discouraged? Do you ever get tired of doing the right thing? Of course you do. It's not easy doing the right thing day after day, month after month, and year after year seemingly without any recognition. Yet, we are to keep and uphold the truth, we are to be just, righteous and holy. When our souls become weary we are to hang on. I like the saying that goes something like this, "when you reach the end of your rope tie a knot and hang on." I know the rougher the trial, or the harder the temptation, the more I tighten my grip on God. It is expressed this way in the New Testament, *Galatians 6:9 "And let us not be weary in well doing: for in due season we shall reap, if we faint not."* It's approximately 700 B.C. in these verses and God is telling the Jews, "Hang on I'm about to reveal my Son to you. I've told you about Him and what He will do and the things He will suffer. He is My salvation, He is My righteousness." This is not only a promise to Isaiah's generation, but to every generation of Jews until the birth of Messiah. You see, the Bible being, a book of faith, hope and trust, would be just as meaningful to the next generation as the previous one until the promise was fulfilled. Can we apply this to our own generation? Absolutely, Jesus gave the promise of His return to His people 2,000 years ago. That promise has been just as precious to each succeeding generation. And one day He will fulfill it with us as well. There is also a special blessing to the person who keeps the faith, doesn't weaken and keeps on doing the right thing, a special promise to those who keep honoring the Lord on the Sabbath and who don't become weak, turning from the right to the wrong to do evil deeds. The blessing is, being taken to the mountaintop, and finding joy in the house of the Lord. Are you living in joy? Have you been to the mountaintop? Just hang on.

Meditation Fifty-Seven

Only the Good Die Young

The righteous perisheth, and no man layeth it to heart: and merciful men are taken away, none considering that the righteous is taken away from the evil to come. He shall enter into peace: they shall rest in their beds, each one walking in his uprightness. For thus saith the high and lofty One that inhabiteth eternity, whose name is Holy; I dwell in the high and holy place, with him also that is of a contrite and humble spirit, to revive the spirit of the humble, and to revive the heart of the contrite ones. Isaiah 57:1, 2 & 15

You know that old saying, "only the good die young?" There is some credence to that. We see in Isaiah's day that many of the righteous, God fearing people were dying but no one really cared. I look around at our world today and more often than not, fewer and fewer of the righteous are mourned over, as a matter of fact much of this evil world rejoices over the death of a righteous person. As far as the world is concerned we are just one more thorn out of their sides, and once the church has been removed from this earth, how many do you think will mourn the loss of a righteous man? Have you ever wondered why so many of what we would consider young people are martyred, or by some other means die at a young age? Here we are told that righteous people are taken out of this world to spare them from having to witness and contend with all its evil. I don't know about you, but in my career in the criminal justice system, I've seen far too many evil things, things that still haunt me to this day. If God would remove me from this world tomorrow, it would bring me nothing but peace and comfort to be in the presence of my Lord, *II Corinthians 5:1 & 8 "For we know that if our earthly house of this tabernacle were dissolved, we have a building of God, an house not made with hands, eternal in the heavens. We are confident, I say, and willing rather to be absent from the body, and to be present with the Lord."*

So then part of the answer to the question as to why some good, Godly people die young is to spare them the heartbreak of having to face all the evil of this world.

Meditation Fifty-Eight

Too Fast or to Fast

Wherefore have we fasted, say they, and thou seest not? wherefore have we afflicted our soul, and thou takest no knowledge? Behold, in the day of your fast ye find pleasure, and exact all your labours. Behold, ye fast for strife and debate, and to smite with the fist of wickedness: ye shall not fast as ye do this day, to make your voice to be heard on high. Is not this the fast that I have chosen? to loose the bands of wickedness, to undo the heavy burdens, and to let the oppressed go free, and that ye break every yoke? Is it not to deal thy bread to the hungry, and that thou bring the poor that are cast out to thy house? when thou seest the naked, that thou cover him; and that thou hide not thyself from thine own flesh? Isaiah 58:3, 4, 6 & 7

We often snivel and whine to God because He doesn't act the way we think He is suppose to act. Part of the problem, of course, is that we are doing the right thing but for the wrong reason. The complaint of the people here is, they were doing all the right things and God was ignoring them. You may have made the same complaint. Have you ever just stopped for a minute and evaluated why you are doing what you do? Why do you go to church? Why do you tithe? Why do you fast? Is what you're doing changing your life and your heart? Or are you still filled with strife, contention, greed, lust or un-forgiveness and bitterness? The Lord then describes to us the fast He wants us to have. It is a soul searching fast, a fast in which we humble ourselves before the Lord. We can expand this and use it to evaluate everything we do in our lives as Christians. The type of fasting, serving and giving the Lord has chosen for us is humbling. This is the type of fast that delivers you from sin. This is the type of fast that lifts heavy burdens, that frees the oppressed and breaks the yoke of bondage. Not the type of fast you may be doing now. A true fast will change you as a person after you have confronted yourself and your sin in the presence of God and His holiness. This is the type of fast that will have you turning away from self and turning towards others. Becoming less self-centered, kinder, and gentler, you begin to seek out ways to reach out and provide for the needs of others, and in so doing show forth the light of Christ.

Meditation Fifty-Nine

I'm Not Deaf

Behold, the LORD'S hand is not shortened, that it cannot save; neither his ear heavy, that it cannot hear: But your iniquities have separated between you and your God, and your sins have hid his face from you, that he will not hear. Isaiah 59:1 & 2

Sometimes I think we believe God has become weak in His old age. I know, I know God is ageless but still we act that way. So God is just letting us know that He is as powerful as He has always been. And just as able to intervene in the affairs of men. And He hasn't gotten hard of hearing either. Well then, if the problem is not with God, who is it with? As usual the problem is with us. We allow our sins and our evil deeds to separate us from God, in so much that He hears He just doesn't listen. But then it has always been that way. King David knew this, *Psalm 66:18 "If I regard iniquity in my heart, the Lord will not hear me:"* The people then knew it, just as you and I know it today, from *Proverbs 28:9 "He that turneth away his ear from hearing the law, even his prayer shall be abomination."* So when we pray, and our prayers don't seem to get any higher than the ceiling, the first place we need to look is at our own life, because personal sin inhibits God from answering our prayers. Here's a simple illustration, you're a parent, you have a child, and you tell your child to pick up his room. After a few minutes you check in on him to see if he's doing what he was told. You open the door, stand in the doorway and look around; the room is still a mess with your child playing in the middle of it. He senses your presence, turns around and asks you to buy him a new toy. What would your response be? Now think about the Father child relationship you have with God. Also you may be praying about a local, regional, or national issue. You have to take into account the spiritual relationship of that area as well. God is not going to answer your prayers if you are in a sin drenched, backslidden, condition. Unless, of course, it is a humble prayer of repentance for forgiveness!

Meditation Sixty

Rise and Shine

Arise, shine; for thy light is come, and the glory of the LORD is risen upon thee. For, behold, the darkness shall cover the earth, and gross darkness the people: but the LORD shall arise upon thee, and his glory shall be seen upon thee. And the Gentiles shall come to thy light, and kings to the brightness of thy rising. Isaiah 60:1-3

Rise and shine! Did you realize that every time you told someone that, you were using a Biblical phrase? Before I get too carried away with an application, I should probably put these verses in their proper future, historical perspective. Sounds like an oxymoron, I assure you its not. This whole chapter is in reference to the Jews in the early days of the Millennium, just after the seven years of tribulation, and the arrival of Jesus. But verse 1 can be applied to believers in the church age as well. We need to arise and shine, get up and let the light of Jesus shine through us to a lost and dying world, because the light of the world has come, and as believers His glory shines on us and dwells in us. Now let's go "back to the future." Both spiritual darkness and actual darkness will be upon the earth during the seven years of tribulation under the Antichrist. There will be one third less light from the sun, moon and stars. Not only will there be one third less light but it will be daylight for one third less time, *Revelation 8:12 "And the fourth angel sounded, and the third part of the sun was smitten, and the third part of the moon, and the third part of the stars; so as the third part of them was darkened, and the day shone not for a third part of it, and the night likewise."* Smoke will fill the sky from volcanoes and cracks in the earth, as well as the pit, *Revelation 9:2 "And he opened the bottomless pit; and there arose a smoke out of the pit, as the smoke of a great furnace; and the sun and the air were darkened by reason of the smoke of the pit."* Then Jesus will return as He said He would, and the light of His physical glory as well as the light of His spiritual glory will shine upon the earth and through the Jews. All the Gentile nations of the world will see the light of the Lord and know where He is setting up shop, in Jerusalem, and will come to the light. You don't have to wait. You can come to the light, Jesus, right now.

Meditation Sixty-One

Two Come Together

The Spirit of the Lord GOD is upon me; because the LORD hath anointed me to preach good tidings unto the meek; he hath sent me to bind up the brokenhearted, to proclaim liberty to the captives, and the opening of the prison to them that are bound; To proclaim the acceptable year of the LORD, and the day of vengeance of our God; to comfort all that mourn; To appoint unto them that mourn in Zion, to give unto them beauty for ashes, the oil of joy for mourning, the garment of praise for the spirit of heaviness; that they might be called trees of righteousness, the planting of the LORD, that he might be glorified. Isaiah 61:1-3

In these three verses we see the two advents of Jesus coming together. The first advent is when God became man and was born of a virgin. The Second Advent is when Jesus comes back to earth with His saints, you and I, and His holy angels, not to be a sacrifice but to be a King. As you read verse one to the first comma in verse two, you will notice that these words are straight out of the mouth of Jesus, words spoken by Him through His prophet Isaiah 700 years before He was that child born in a manager. Seven hundred years before they were recorded in the fourth chapter of Luke. Jesus would lay claim to being the Messiah of God early in His ministry. The Holy Spirit of His Father had merged with His mortal frame, and anointed Him for His ministry of peace, healing, salvation and freedom to mankind. And now is the appropriate time for reconciliation with His Father through faith in Him. Very quickly though the first advent merges into the second, a time of vengeance that will come thousands of years later, a time we call the seven years of tribulation. This vengeance will deal with both the unbelieving Jew and the unbelieving Gentile, who will choose to follow the Antichrist. But what of the believing Jews and Gentiles who will be brought through seven years of hell on earth. Jesus is going to care for His saved remnant that He will bring through the fire. The sorrow and grief they will wear on their heads will be replaced by a garland wreath of beauty. Weeping and mourning will be replaced by the holy anointing of joy and their ragged, tattered clothes will be replaced by a white garment of praise. And so whether we are taken out or brought through, we will all be comforted.

Meditation Sixty-Two

For Zion's Sake

For Zion's sake will I not hold my peace, and for Jerusalem's sake I will not rest, until the righteousness thereof go forth as brightness, and the salvation thereof as a lamp that burneth. And the Gentiles shall see thy righteousness, and all kings thy glory: and thou shalt be called by a new name, which the mouth of the LORD shall name. Behold, the LORD hath proclaimed unto the end of the world, Say ye to the daughter of Zion, Behold, thy salvation cometh; behold, his reward is with him, and his work before him. And they shall call them, The holy people, The redeemed of the LORD: and thou shalt be called, Sought out, A city not forsaken. Isaiah 62:1, 2 11 & 12

Israel is a very secular state and there are limited numbers of Messianic Jews. However, my pro-Jewish stand allows me to encourage Christians. God made promises to the Jews in His Holy Word, to the nation Israel, and to the city of Jerusalem and it is God's intent to keep them all. If He broke even one of these promises He might break the promises He has made to you and me as Christians, then where would our security be? The Lord is not going to keep still concerning His people. He's going to keep working on them and with them until they become the people He intended them to be. Originally, the Jews were to be God's brightness to the world in matters concerning salvation. In other words if you wanted to know God you would go to a Jew to learn how. Also the world has never seen the glory of Israel the way it was meant to be, the closest it ever came was during the reign of King Solomon in I Kings 10. In the mean time what are we to do as Christians? We are to proclaim the Gospel, of course. Jesus gave the commission in *Matthew 28: 19, "Go ye therefore, and teach all nations, baptizing them in the name of the Father, and of the Son, and of the Holy Ghost:"* and *Acts 1:8 "But ye shall receive power, after that the Holy Ghost is come upon you: and ye shall be witnesses unto me both in Jerusalem, and in all Judaea, and in Samaria, and unto the uttermost part of the earth."* This is the fulfillment of Isaiah 62:11. The world's opinion of Jews and of Israel is rather low. Many nations would exterminate all Hebrews. However, for a thousand years the Jews will be known as the Holy people of God, the redeemed of the Lord. The nations of the world will seek them out for their knowledge of God and Jesus will reign from Jerusalem.

Meditation Sixty-Three

Mighty to Save

Who is this that cometh from Edom, with dyed garments from Bozrah? this that is glorious in his apparel, travelling in the greatness of his strength? I that speak in righteousness, mighty to save. Wherefore art thou red in thine apparel, and thy garments like him that treadeth in the winefat? I have trodden the winepress alone; and of the people there was none with me: for I will tread them in mine anger, and trample them in my fury; and their blood shall be sprinkled upon my garments, and I will stain all my raiment. Isaiah 63:1-3

Here is another picture of Christ returning to the world as the conquering Warrior King: arrayed in regal robes instead of a lowly carpenter's garments and traveling in royal splendor with heaven's armies accompanying Him. He will be coming in His righteousness and power. Jesus will be marching into Jerusalem from the southeastern end of Israel looking like someone who has been stomping grapes in a vat as was the custom in the day that Isaiah was written. This is not a pretty picture, and many Christians don't want to be associated with a God of wrath. Yet, capital crimes require capital punishment for justice to be done, *Genesis 9:6: "Whoso sheddeth man's blood, by man shall his blood be shed: for in the image of God made he man." Revelation 14:19 & 20: "And the angel thrust in his sickle into the earth, and gathered the vine of the earth, and cast it into the great winepress of the wrath of God. And the winepress was trodden without the city, and blood came out of the winepress, even unto the horse bridles, by the space of a thousand and six hundred furlongs." Revelation 19:11-16: "And I saw heaven opened, and behold a white horse; and he that sat upon him was called Faithful and True, and in righteousness he doth judge and make war. His eyes were as a flame of fire, and on his head were many crowns; and he had a name written, that no man knew, but he himself. And he was clothed with a vesture dipped in blood: and his name is called The Word of God. And the armies which were in heaven followed him upon white horses, clothed in fine linen, white and clean. And out of his mouth goeth a sharp sword, that with it he should smite the nations: and he shall rule them with a rod of iron: and he treadeth the winepress of the fierceness and wrath of Almighty God."* Jesus is a righteous, holy God and always takes full responsibility for His actions and the pouring out of His wrath. It was He alone that procured salvation for the world, and it is He alone that will judge it.

Meditation Sixty-Four

We Don't Have a Clue

For since the beginning of the world men have not heard, nor perceived by the ear, neither hath the eye seen, O God, beside thee, what he hath prepared for him that waiteth for him. But now, O LORD, thou art our father; we are the clay, and thou our potter; and we all are the work of thy hand. Be not wroth very sore, O LORD, neither remember iniquity for ever: behold, see, we beseech thee, we are all thy people. Isaiah 64:4, 8, 9

As natural beings, even as believers we have only an inkling, the merest glimmer, of what God has in store for us. Have you ever stood on a mountaintop, sat on a seashore, looked out across a desert or wandered through a rainforest? Have you ever heard the screech of an eagle, the scream of a mountain lion, the howling of wolves, or the bellow of a bison? I have, I have seen and heard all of these and many more. On many occasions, my heart has been so moved with awe that tears have flooded my eyes. Yet, the only knowledge I have of heavenly things, is what has been revealed to me in the Word of God by the Spirit of God, *I Corinthians 2:9-10 "But as it is written, Eye hath not seen, nor ear heard, neither have entered into the heart of man, the things which God hath prepared for them that love him. But God hath revealed them unto us by his Spirit: for the Spirit searcheth all things, yea, the deep things of God."* We so limit God. Will the new heavens and new earth be less diverse than this one, a heaven and earth free from the curse of sin and the taint of Satan's evil? Will we be any less able to enjoy these things with a perfect glorified body like the body of our risen Lord and Savior, Jesus? We just don't have a clue, do we? In the mean time let us not forget that not only is God our Creator, He is also our Father and being such we should be submissive and malleable to the hand of our Father, the Potter, and allow Him to make us into what He will. Do you remember back to a time when you were a child? A time when you did something wrong and you asked your dad to not be mad at you? Do you recognize sin in your life and plead for forgiveness before the Father through Jesus the Son, *I John 1:9 "If we confess our sins, he is faithful and just to forgive us our sins, and to cleanse us from all unrighteousness."* Something else we don't have a clue about is the grace and forgiveness of God.

Meditation Sixty-Five

Provision for All

I am sought of them that asked not for me; I am found of them that sought me not: I said, Behold me, behold me, unto a nation that was not called by my name. Therefore thus saith the Lord GOD, Behold, my servants shall eat, but ye shall be hungry: behold, my servants shall drink, but ye shall be thirsty: behold, my servants shall rejoice, but ye shall be ashamed: Behold, my servants shall sing for joy of heart, but ye shall cry for sorrow of heart, and shall howl for vexation of spirit. That he who blesseth himself in the earth shall bless himself in the God of truth; and he that sweareth in the earth shall swear by the God of truth; because the former troubles are forgotten, and because they are hid from mine eyes. For, behold, I create new heavens and a new earth: and the former shall not be remembered, nor come into mind. Isaiah 65: 1, 13, 14, 16 & 17

God is now working with the Gentile nations, pouring out His grace on us. Remember the Jews are God's chosen people. He made them a nation separating them from the world. He gave them a land, a law, and a Lord. We Gentiles were a bunch of heathens. We were not seeking after the one true God yet God was seeking after us. We know this verse applies to us because Paul, a Jew quoted it as applying to us, *Romans 10:19 & 20 "But I say, Did not Israel know? First Moses saith, I will provoke you to jealousy by them that are no people, and by a foolish nation I will anger you. But Esaias is very bold, and saith, I was found of them that sought me not; I was made manifest unto them that asked not after me."* By the time we get to verses 13 and 14 we are back to the contrast of the believing and unbelieving Jews of the tribulation. But the principle applies to all who believe and trust in the Lord and His provision, "My servants shall eat, My servants shall drink, My servants shall rejoice, My servants shall sing." If we are to be blessed in the earth then we are to bless ourselves in the God of truth. And as we bless ourselves by embracing the truth of God and the God of the truth, our former troubles will fade from our lives and disappear from before our eyes. Once again we have been given the promise of a new heaven and a new earth. You know as natural beings, we often wax nostalgic about the past, remembering it better than it was. But in the heavens and earth to come no one will want to go back and the only found memory you will have was of the day you were saved. This new heaven and new earth will be so fabulous and filled with wonders that this one will be forgotten.

Meditation Sixty-Six

God, in a Box?

Thus saith the LORD, The heaven is my throne, and the earth is my footstool: where is the house that ye build unto me? and where is the place of my rest? For all those things hath mine hand made, and all those things have been, saith the LORD: but to this man will I look, even to him that is poor and of a contrite spirit, and trembleth at my word. Isaiah 66:1 & 2

We seem to always want to put God in a box. We like to set Him on a shelf or put Him in a box, with our other toys. And when we get around to it we will turn His crank so God pops out and usually we are surprised, a God with a big smile on His face that wavers back and forth. We say a little prayer to our God in the box hoping He will grant us our wish and when we're done we stuff Him back down in His little box, snap the lid on and put Him away until the next time we want to be entertained. But in these first couple of verses of this last chapter of Isaiah, God takes the time to straighten us out. God is not in a box! His throne is in heaven. The heaven as in the sky that the clouds float by in, the heaven as in the farthest reaches of outer space, and the heaven as in the celestial, eternal, spiritual dimension. The earth is little more than a footstool to God. Stephen quotes these words just before he is stoned to death and goes to meet God, *Acts 7:48-50 "Howbeit the most High dwelleth not in temples made with hands; as saith the prophet, Heaven is my throne, and earth is my footstool: what house will ye build me? saith the Lord: or what is the place of my rest? Hath not my hand made all these things?"* God cannot be contained in a building. The wisest man the world has ever known, besides Jesus, knew this and said so in, *I Kings 8:27 "[27]But will God indeed dwell on the earth? behold, the heaven and heaven of heavens cannot contain thee; how much less this house that I have builded?"* Although God cannot be contained in a box, a building, or even the known universe He will come in and dwell with, abide with and inhabit a certain type of person. It is not the type of person who wants to turn God's crank or wants a genie in a lamp. No, instead it is the person who comes before God with a humble, broken heart, fully aware that he is a poor sinner in need of the grace of God. A person who reads these words and trembles before his Creator, it is this type of person that God elevates to friendship and son-ship, to never leave or forsake throughout all the ages of time and into eternity. Are you that person?